Saratoga Lives

Michael Hare

ISBN-13: 978-0-6151-5440-4

For information contact:

Equipoise Press
PO Box 3046
Saratoga Springs, NY 12866

FOREWORD

Saratoga. A name synonymous with mineral water, a Revolutionary War battlefield, Victorian splendor, ornate casinos, artistic illumination and hard-charging thoroughbreds. Its people: the intrepid, the eminent, the scoundrels and thugs, elitists, visionaries, charlatans and cynics, the braggarts, hustlers and heretics, have for over two centuries shaped Saratoga. Here, some of those characters, real and imagined, give voice to their *Saratoga Lives.*

JANUARY 6, 1801

MRS. GIDEON PUTNAM

A wild wood it is,
Filled with moose, deer, and in that
Grove of pines this morning
A bear looked at me and sneered
Before ambling off to
Search for food.
Yet Gideon contends this is the place he wants
To stay:
The forest is huge, the Indians are leaving,
And that curious water gurgling up from the
Ground has what he calls "potential."
So we live in a wooden cabin by a clearing
Near what someday may become a street.
I tend to the cooking and the children and
Listen to Gideon when he comes home, and
Tells me his dreams of a place where
Someday people will sojourn, and live,
And prosper.

LINDEN BEATS

Give me a gun over a tomahawk any time
And I'll show you what killing's all about.
I hunt for possum, coon, squirrels: measly varmints
With no business breathing.
When I butcher a deer or buck
I'll eat well for days.
But the best prey of all are those damned worthless
Redskins.
Once years ago I sensed
Twigs cracking behind me.
I turned and through the trees a
Redskin yelped a war-cry and
Lunged at me waving his tomahawk.
I fired and nailed him square in the chest.
When he fell at my feet I put the muzzle on his neck
And finished him off.
He never looked better than when his head was
Ripped from his body, his hand still clutching
That useless tomahawk.

ALEXANDER BRYAN

Gideon is the planner, the
Visionary, but it was my ingenuity that
Championed the British defeat.
I earned the trust of Burgoyne by
Disclosing information that could be of no harm
To Gates, and met with him that September,
When they had crossed the Hudson and were
Advancing on Bemis Heights.
Burgoyne must have been suspicious,
Because when I departed two men trailed me
Before I eluded them in the forest.
I made it to camp, and told Gates of
Burgoyne's march.
Gates and Arnold were prepared, Burgoyne was
Routed, and the seeds of
America were planted.

SARAH EDWARDS

Who would have thought that
Leaving my neighborhood near
Oxford to come to an outpost called Saratoga
Could be such a godsend?
While Doradeen pines for the old land and
Doanda caters to Gideon,
I look at the natives and find myself piqued
By peculiar thoughts.
I have a wish to leave Arthur and our cabin
And stake out my chances alone in the wilderness,
To see what a savage would do with a
Woman well-bred and educated.
At times I am severely tested to hold my desires
In abeyance.
I succeed, and instead achieve
Transports with Arthur,
Or alone.

DORADEEN SUTLIFF

When Anthony brought me here from England
He rhapsodized of abundant trees,
Scenic mountains, crystalline streams
And mysterious, life-enhancing water.
I came with him and found
Nothing but muck, slime and dirt.
The men hunt and we women
Stay behind and hope no Indians
Come our way.
I sit in this hovel with Sarah Edwards
And Doanda Putnam, and suspire for the day
I return to England.

ANTHONY SUTLIFF

A man is master of his domain, whether
It be on the streets of London or
A tiny settlement called Saratoga.
I will remind Doradeen of
Her vows to love, honor and
Obey.
Gideon and Doanda will spend
The rest of their lives here,
As will Doradeen and I.
If she brings up the matter again,
I will tell her categorically:
We will not return to England.

ROBERT ELLIS

Thomas Jefferson or Aaron Burr?
At the height of the war
Eleanor and I came to Saratoga by oxcart.
I built a cabin, the Mohawks retreated, and
The nightly howl of the wolves
Drifted into our dreams.
A Virginian, enamored of the French Revolution?
One child came, then a second and third.
Eleanor nursed them, raised them
And cooked for them
While I farmed, became a merchant
And then a representative in government.
Or a New Yorker gripped by mercantile exchange?
In the cabin I see pots and kettles,
Mittens and blankets,
Gingham dresses, boots and shoes.
At meals I want to speak to her
While at night I believe I can touch her.
Then I recall how today the children,
Nearly fully grown,
Huddled together while
I shoveled away the snow
By the marker.
And I'm told I must decide:
Jefferson or Burr?

SAMUEL PASTORE

Fighting alongside Benedict Arnold in
The battle of Saratoga,
Rising to First Lieutenant,
Moving to Albany following the war,
Then to New York,
Participating in the creation of
The Federal Reserve, I have helped to mold
Our nation's affairs.
A member of the Federalist Party,
I actively supported President Adams, and
Consider the Alien and Sedition Act
An effective tool to counter treason.
Adams has lost the election, and the choice is
Jefferson or Burr.
I have corresponded with Robert Ellis,
Urging him to use his influence thoughtfully.
If the Federalists can no longer rule,
Aaron Burr will suffice.

HIRAM BEAM

Given the choice, why does man always choose
The mysteries of the untested over the certitude
Of the known? Why do Gideon Putnam,
Benjamin Risley and their confederates
Struggle to make a settlement in a place of
Inscrutable waters, ten miles from
The mighty Hudson?
Why did the revolutionaries spurn a noble King
To test a form a government
Never before attempted in civilization?
I will make a prediction:
America is as doomed as
The Indian Nations, and when
Albany becomes a leading port under
The Union Jack, Saratoga will be remembered
Only as a failed experiment.

JANE BEAM

Hiram has never accepted the rout of
England, and the actions of
Alexander Bryan cause him
To particularly loathe Saratoga.
He constantly states that
Seeking the unknown leads only
To regret.
Then at day's end he is
On his knees, imploring help from a
Deity that no one anywhere
Has ever seen.

PERCIVAL FARTHINGHAM

As adjutant to General Burgoyne
I reaped the glory of our triumphant advance,
Rattling the insipid foe at Ticonderoga and
At points south.
The engagement at Bemis Heights was to be
No more than a skirmish that would barely slow
Our inexorable march to Albany.
There the fiends came at us in wave after wave,
Bloodying the fields with
The King's army, forcing us into
Abject surrender.
Following the battle I was relieved
Of my military rank and returned to
My estate in London.
Condemnation on the colonies!
May their baneful country
Rot from the violence
From which issued its hateful breath!

BENJAMIN RISLEY

My daughter relinquished the wealth and ease
Of our family estate in Hartford to marry
A descendent of Israel Putnam.
I granted Gideon permission when he pledged
The welfare of Doanda would eclipse
All other concerns.
When Doanda's letters began arriving
I feared stories of privation, discomfort
And unhappiness.
Instead, she described
Her husband's devotion, the resolution to establish
A harmonious community, and their desire to
Raise a family.
And they would be honored
If I would join them.
Here in Saratoga
I advise and counsel Gideon, assist in the
Rearing of my grandchildren,
And live in deference to the
Will of God.

JACOB WINSLOW

My business dealings with Benjamin Risley
In Hartford were mutually satisfactory,
And I consented to meet with he and his
Son-in-law whose purpose was construction of
An inn, for which they required capital.
I traveled north through denser and denser
Wilderness, until I arrived in Saratoga.
There I discovered wild game,
Scattered savages, mud-caked huts, wooden
Shanties, and foul water.
Neither Benjamin nor Mr. Putnam
Could persuade me to invest.
Returning to Hartford,
I passed through an already established hamlet
Where respectable structures
And accommodations for travelers exist.
I will express to Benjamin that prospects
For development in Ballston Spa far outweigh
Any opportunity in his
Roughhewn hinterland.

CHRISTIANA BARHYTE

I never knew where he was that day;
He may have been fishing,
Throwing the fish he caught
Back into the lake, or talking in Dutch
To his geese and chickens.
I was in the loghouse,
The babe asleep in the cradle,
When in walked the bear.
It would have been faster had I
Grabbed the musket, but I'd been
Cutting up pork with a case-knife,
And that's what I used.
When the babe started to cry
My resolve hardened,
And when it was done
I became aware we'd have more than pork
In the next weeks.
Later, I knew he was coming
By the sound of Dutch Psalms
Echoing through the forest.

NICK BLAKE

I knifed a wretch under
Big Ben and sliced open a
Harlot within sight of
The Tower.
Then I got onboard a ship,
Got to New York and ended up
In Saratoga.
Gideon Putnam buys me spirits
At Risley's Tavern,
Arthur Edwards
Gives me corn from his field,
And my cabin is sealed tight
Against the winter wind.
I hear talk of
Life, Liberty and the Pursuit of
Happiness.
Listen to Nick Blake:
In Saratoga
You can get all three.

CRYMPTON DOUGLAS

Clearing the land,
Clearing the land.
Oak, pine, hemlock,
Maple, elm, chestnut,
Felled by axes.
Bramble, thorns, brush
Hacked away,
Laying bare
Dirt, clay and mud
In what they call
The Lower Village.
Gideon Putnam
Overseeing it all,
Telling us that
Clearing the land
Will provide space
For an American
Eden.

JULY 1, 1879

GRAND UNION COURT, SARATOGA SPRINGS, N.Y.

MADAME SLOVAKETY

My forebearers fled Russia and
Peter the Great.
They brought cosmic wisdom
To the New World and
Jars of rubles to our new home
On Circular Street in Saratoga.
I can see a man's future
In the lines of his hand
And know at once if he will
Succeed in commerce
Or in love.
The casinos here
Don't admit women.
So I tell men I know
The right times to make the right bets.
When they win (which they usually do)
I take twenty percent.
Farley Payne won ten thousand dollars
One day last year,
And left Saratoga without telling me
Or giving me my share.
Is it a surprise they found him dead
In New York City the following week,
Poisoned by cheap vodka?

LIONEL PAYNE

My brother's unfortunate death is an
Important lesson to me.
After winning thousands at the Casino in Saratoga
He traveled to New York,
Where he took up with Lucille Pendergast,
The wife of the railroad tycoon
(They had met in Saratoga the summer before).
Well, Mr. Pendergast caught on, and
Being in a position where a scandal wouldn't do,
He ordered Tommy Hellman,
The barkeep at the hotel where they stayed,
To doctor his drink.
So Farley died and Mr. Pendergast paid Tommy
For his work, and left his wife.
I learned all this from Lucille.
Oh, my lesson?
If you have an identical twin
And play the odds accordingly,
You double your chance for success!

ELIZA HYDE

Such a gaudy masquerade last week
In the Congress Hall ballroom!
Napoleon guided Josephine with mincing stride
To a far corner; Cleopatra, wearing a diamond tiara,
Appeared with Marc Antony;
And with a roaring laugh entered Henry VIII,
Displaying his bride, Anne Boleyn.
As Joan of Arc I danced with
Byron, Voltaire and Alexander the Great
Until the playing of the last Strauss waltz.
From a table Benjamin Franklin
Kept watching me, tilting back his head
As if trying to unmask me through his bifocals.
It appeared he would approach when the
Violins and horns sounded again,
And I was conducted away
By Wolfgang Mozart!

ZACK ZAYNE

Allow me to announce that Saratoga's finest
Haberdashery is open for business on Broadway!
Gentlemen, step in and find your needs attended to
With courteous efficiency.
Silk cravats of dazzling color, leather gloves
In brown and black, buckles, boots and linen
Trousers, hats and razors, fobs and watches,
Cotton shirts and woolen overcoats
Of the highest quality abound!
Tarry at Zayne's Haberdashery and
Leave with the accouterments designed for
The Saratoga gentleman
With aplomb!

HERMAN WHITTENBERG

My father worked with Dr. Clarke,
Ably assisting in the creation of
Congress Park and the bottling of the
Congress Spring.
I have made Saratoga Springs my lifetime home,
Blessed with a dutiful wife and
Respectful children.
Pains in my stomach and sides
Have lately become unbearable and the
Diagnosis is internal bleeding and growths
That will spell my mortal undoing.
This, at the age of forty-one, and
A lifetime replete with
Saratoga's inexhaustible variety of
Mineral water!

GENEVIEVE WINTHROP

I travel with my husband from New York
To Saratoga each season by private carriage,
For I cannot abide the noise and grime
Of the train.
I prefer the suites of the
The Clarendon, where manicured grounds
Lead directly to the Washington Spring, and
I partake of the other waters only
When the crowds have dispersed.
Thaddeus instructs the servants
To properly arrange my velvet pillows
And see that we are not disturbed
Between ten at night and eight in the morning.
Last year the Billingtons inquired
If they might vacation with us.
I could only laugh at their impudence,
And take pride that I
Refuse to cheapen
The Spa.

NATE KNOX

Saratoga must be one giant pot of honey because
They come in swarms every summer.
They buzz and circle as I lug their trunks and
Unpack their suits and vests and finery.
The Queen's attendants are frequently derelict:
"Could you procure a fan for my wife
So she can keep cool on the veranda?"
The nectar from the flower is sometimes acrid:
"Could you take this back and ask the
Chef to cook the meat so it's tender?"
The hive is often cramped and narrow:
"Can you arrange for the carriage to pick us up
At seven tomorrow for our ride
To the lake?"
In September it's time to
Pollinate somewhere else,
And they throw me a nickel or fifteen cents
Just to show off their stingers.

CECIL RUPPLEHOUSE

Jaundice, dyspepsia, failing appetite,
Rheumatism, gout, scrofula, paralysis, and
Some species of dropsy:
The guidebook says the mineral springs
Combat them all.
Bah!
Well dressed fools sipping and
Grimacing would be a perfect
New act for P.T. Barnum's
Circus!

ASA CUTTER

We live in the finest nation in the world,
In one of its most picturesque locales:
Just ask the nouveau riche here in Saratoga.
And the process by which we
Elect our president is eminently fair and
Proper, particularly in the south:
Just ask the republicans.
And the working classes
Are well cared for and attended to:
Just ask them if you can find where they live.
So Saratoga struts and preens, the
Cock-of-the-walk in the great big farm
Called the United States.
I've already purchased my admission ticket
To witness the events when Saratoga's
Hogs and goats step beyond
The farmyard gate.

ANGELINE DAMASK

Rodney was eager to serve the
Cause of the Union and enlisted
Two weeks after our Wedding Day,
Over my objections.
Rodney came back to Saratoga in a casket
Within a month, shot by accident from behind
By a fellow Union soldier.
I married Floyd Damask after the war,
And we named our son Rodney.
When my son fights with his playmates,
And learns how to shoot,
And tells me Stonewall Jackson
Should have killed his own troops
One by one with a sword,
I can only fight to hold back the tears
While I brush back his hair.

RORY DODGE

I didn't think Nate Ross would mind
If I stood on the steps of Village Hall
And denounced the British Empire
As an affront to 19th Century
Civilization.
When I shouted,
"Barbarism in the name of
Union Jack is no better
Than brutality in the cause of the
Crusades!" Nate yelled back,
"Barbarism in the name of
Freedom is the pre-eminent right
Of Englishmen!"
And he fired his pistol at me.
The bullet whizzed by my ear,
And while arguing about
Ireland over beer and whiskey,
Nate was bludgeoned to death
By his neighbor,
Shamus O'Shaunessey.

OLIVER PENBROKE

Before I worked at the new United States Hotel,
I worked at the head desk of the Grand Union.
"Mr. and Mrs. Powell? Misses Knapp and Collins?
Attorney Howe? A boy will assist you."
The United States stands at the corner of
Broadway and Division. Note the
Axminster carpets, carved walnut and marble
Furniture, golden chandeliers,
And the frescoed ballroom ceiling
Twenty-six feet high.
"Mr. Siegel, your rooms are ready."

ISABELLE SOULER

Go ahead, you far-sighted leaders and businessmen
Of Saratoga, build, build, build!
Build your hotels five, six, ten stories high
All up and down Broadway,
Let them stretch for miles!
You, Henry Hilton, don't stop with the
Grand Union, buy more property, build hotels
On Caroline, Regent, Phila!
Then tell me what happened to the United States
In 1865, Congress Hall in 1866 and
The Grand Central in 1874.
And I'll tell you what happened in 1811:
My grandfather, Barney Souler, helping build
Congress Hall, killed by the collapse
Of heavy timber.
Gideon Putnam, by my
Grandfather's side, struck down,
Dead within two years,
While all around they kept right on:
Build, build, build!

MOSES HIRSCH

Mr. Lincoln and the
Abolitionists freed the Negro
From the white man, but when will the
Jew be freed from the
Christian?
I have stayed at the Grand Union each year,
Willingly paying their escalating fees,
Only to be told as I entered
On the day before the Sabbath,
"We can no longer accommodate you.
This is a gentile establishment."
It appears the new proprietor,
Mr. Hilton, no longer wants us in his
Modernized behemoth.
The Old Testament speaks of a hell
A million times the size of any hotel.
May Mr. Hilton find his accommodations there
Abominable, loathsome and
Ineluctable.

JUDITH HIRSCH

Moses has earned his time away from New York City
And the bank. Each day he pours over accounts,
Rates of interest, investors' fees, treasury notes
And government bonds.
He returns home weary, but never once
Has neglected me,
On Holidays he never fails to distribute gifts
To the bank clerks, and when funds are needed
At Temple for improvements, the first check
Always comes from Moses.
To see him at the Grand Union last week,
Shaking as might be expected for a
Seventy year old man, was nearly too much for me.
Mr. McCaffrey keeps his rooms
In his small, new hotel on Broadway
Open to all.
This summer my husband and I
Will read Scripture and pray to God
From our room in the Adelphi.

CLYDE HARRIS

The judge, he says,
"Harris, get my coat," and
"Harris, fetch the carriage," and
"Harris, whip those damned horses!"
And we bustle from the Grand Union
To North Broadway so he can supervise
Construction of what he calls "Woodlawn."
Then he runs around waving his arms,
Yelling at the bricklayers and
Carpenters, and he tracks down the
Boss, "Get your ass moving!"
Then he shouts at me,
"Harris, the carriage!"
And back we fly to the Grand Union.
And I says to myself,
I'll be damned if someday somebody
Don't arrange an accident.
And, I says to myself,
Wouldn't Woodlawn be a nice name
For a burial ground?

JUDGE HENRY HILTON

Ha!
When I met the old man in New York I knew
I'd found my avenue to riches.
He sought camaraderie; I was compliant.
He turned to me for advice; I obliged. He required
Friendship; I spent time with him to the exclusion
Of all else.
I watched his mind slip, saw his body decay,
And as executor after his passing
I achieved my reward:
The Grand Union Hotel.
There it stands on Broadway like a leviathan
While to the north my immense estate
Is being built.
In the decades and centuries to come
They will gape at my hotel
And Woodlawn,
Replete with gardens and sculpture,
Will be the American version
Of the Louvre.
Therefore, it is decreed that my present
Fame and fortune will be passed on
In perpetuity.

MORTIMER CAGE

Alexander Stewart, your judgment failed you
In the end. In New York City I managed your
Department stores,
Assisted in your purchase of factories,
And helped you create Garden City,
Thinking myself indispensable.
Your wealth accumulated while my stipend
Barely grew; you lived with your wife in grander
And grander homes while I lived in my
Bachelor's flat; I warned that the purchase of
The Grand Union was ill advised
Considering your age and declining health.
In time my opinions ceased to be irrefutable,
Replaced by the bluster and insolence of that
Toady of Tammany Hall.
Alexander Stewart, was he even there to watch
When they laid you down
Beneath a slab of granite?

MRS. ALEXANDER STEWART

Alexander never would have wished for this
To happen. That odious man, Hilton, each year
Became more and more familiar, spending all day
With him in the office, dining with us,
Discussing business and the law for hours on end.
When Alexander took ill, where else could he turn?
And when he died, did Hilton grieve?
No! He had the papers all prepared,
I signed them, and the amount
I was paid cannot approach the value of
The Grand Union.
And with his fortune I understand he's
Building himself a castle in the woods.
Thinking about him brings only agitation.
Instead, I will prize my memories with
Alexander, here on Thirty Second Street, where
Most of my neighbors have never heard
Of Saratoga.

MATILDA RAPPAPORT

Yesterday I kissed my mother goodbye
For today I am wed to Jonathan.
Holding hands we entered Congress Park
Along the exquisite promenade.
We walked on slate floors through the Arcade
Beside gleaming woodwork showered with
Reflections of violet, ruby and garnet light
And sipped water drawn from
Beneath the earth.
When M. Voullieme removed fresh caramels
From his oven at the end of the Arcade
My appetite awakened.
Jonathan waited to make his purchase
As I looked into the distance to
Deer Lodge, where fawns approach the
Caretaker to be fed hickory nuts
By hand.

AMANDA COLLIER

I stood with the throng on Broadway on that
Summer day in 1849 when from the United States
She set out for the lake in her
Dazzling equipage, preening as if she were
Queen Victoria deigning to suffer her subjects'
Affections.
Then right behind came a second equipage,
Driven by Smith Brill, Caleb Adams
In footman's dress, and in the carriage,
Dressed in women's clothes, his face black as
Charcoal, sat old Tom Camel!
Old Tom curtseyed, fluttered his fan and
Tipped his bonnet, his thick lips
Set in a big smile exposing rows white teeth,
And we all waved and hollered and cheered!
Smith Brill told us later the old lady didn't catch on
Until they reached the lake, and said if she brought
Her gun she'd order them all into the water,
And would have shot anyone who
Disobeyed her orders
To drown.

CATHERINE PETERS

As a little girl I would go to her house on
Circular Street, over my mother's objections,
Thinking it the finest place in the world.
She would serve me toast with
Raspberry jam, tea sweetened with honey, and
Sometimes fresh baked cakes rich with chocolate.
She showed me her pictures as a young woman,
And told story after story of Jumel, Aaron Burr,
And Napoleon, laughing all the while.
She told me that each man wrongly thought he
Could possess her completely, and I wondered
At her words when I came home.
As for me, I married Richard Peters and raised
Three sons and a daughter.
The boys are all grown and married, and
When I talk to Betsy, now seventeen, she hardly
Seems to listen, as if she's hearing a voice
I can only imagine.

GEORGE HARVEY

My lumber business at the intersection of
Division and Walworth had vast potential
At the beginning of the decade.
I lived in Franklin Square and
Provided materials to the builders of
The great hotels. Then the Credit Mobilizer scandal,
The Whiskey Ring scandal, and
Economic depression brought on by
The malfeasance of Grant and by 1876
No one had any use for the French Renaissance style,
Or any money to build.
I closed my business and left
Saratoga where eighty years ago
Gideon Putnam made his fortune doing
The very thing that forces beyond
My control prevented me from
Accomplishing.

MAJOR ROBERT HORNELL

I marched through Georgia with General Sherman,
Our troops setting a swath of fire
To our right and left, destroying
Cotton fields, sheds, houses, trees, and
Whatever southerners happened to be
In our way.
Our conquest was nearly complete when a band
Of disconsolate rebels fired on us
Just outside of Savannah.
I was hit in the gut and fell to the earth.
They eventually put me on a train to
Washington, where the doctors removed the bullet
Along with a kidney and part of my stomach.
No longer able to fight, I came home to Saratoga.
More and more southerners
Are coming here for the season,
Their drawl drowned out by
War whoops, guns and cannons, and cries
Of agonizing death.

MAX ABERCALM

Mucking stables
Dodging kicks
Ducking bites
Smelling like dung.
Working from
Five to ten,
Noon to three
Five to nine,
Six days a week,
And sometimes Sunday.
And my wife complaining
About no money,
Saying sewing is hard
On her eyes.
I don't always feel better
When I hit her,
But usually I don't
Feel no worse.

GAIL ABERCALM

I wish I could do more,
I'm trying to contribute
To our finances,
Not because of him,
But because of Janey.
I want her to live
A satisfactory life.
So I knit and sew
For as many families
As I can.
And he can't understand
That my eyes give way
And lack of money
Makes me nervous
And makes him mad.
When he hits me
I see even less and
Hope that Janey sees
Nothing at all.

LAIRD BROWNELL

In 1841 I was denied the privilege of
Joining the wardens of the
Bethesda Episcopal Church
Because of my youth.
I was therefore unable to voice my opposition to
The acquisition of Rockwell Putnam's property on
Washington Street for construction of our new
House of Worship.
The Church was built at a prodigious cost,
The mortgage was not fully paid for decades,
And the Church is now nearly swallowed whole
By the Grand Union Hotel.
Had I a voice in 1841, we would be
Worshiping today on Temple Hill,
Giving our faithful the
Appropriate opportunity to overlook
The rest of Saratoga.

SANDER CUMMINGS, ESQ.

For a church to succeed in our society,
The hand of the Lord must be assisted by the
Arm of the Law.
A.T. Stewart tried to usurp our property
To make his Grand Union larger in 1873, alleging
We had not perfected title, and our mortgage
Was still unpaid.
We went to court, where I proved title was cleared
In 1841, and the mortgage, after thirty years,
Had been retired.
My efforts earned me the position of
Church warden, where I vigilantly ensure
That all documentation from our vestry
Comports with secular justice.

YANKEE SULLIVAN

English-raised, I arrived in the colonies
Well-versed in the art of pugilistics and the codes of
The Marquis of Queensbury.
On October 12, 1853, I was matched against
Morrisey, and a fouler lout
Never stepped into a ring.
I pummeled him round after round, enduring
Thumbs to my eyes, blows beneath my belt,
Kicks to my shins, and invective
From the drunken crowd.
After thirty-six rounds
I sensed triumph was mine.
He started pointing and shouting at me
From across the ring; the mob surged,
Fists and bottles flew, and the wastrels went
Berserk when the craven referee
Declared the bout over
And him champion.
I returned to England where sport and society
Are civilized, and understand that Morrisey
Turned a quaint little village
Into a haven for derelicts
Like himself.

PAUL FLANDERS

Finding no gold in Frisco
Old Smoke and I came to New York
Where I taught the brawler to box.
His bare-knuckle defeats of Sullivan and Heenan
Paralleled our ascension from the political back alley
To the side of Boss Tweed, culminating with the
Murder of the Know-Nothing, Poole,
At the hands of The Dead Rabbits.
In Saratoga he opened his ledgers on faro and stakes.
Gracefully sparring with tycoons and socialites,
Sleek, elegant, tactful, he became a married man,
A father.
Twice elected to Congress, twice elected to
The State Senate, revered, yet nearly diffident,
I watched him absorb a thunderous blow
When his son succumbed to fatal disease.
Then grieving with his wife
From a room in the Adelphi,
Not yet fifty years old,
With manifest dignity,
He capitulated.

DANNY O'KEEFE

So yer looking to gamble at Mr. Morrisey's
Saratoga Club, are ye?
Yeah, Mr. Morrisey's passed on, but his
Rules haven't died.
You don't look like Mr. Vanderbilt, let's see
Yer credentials.
What d'ya mean, you only got
Fifty dollars in yer pocket?
No, there ain't no credit for no gentleman
By yer name.
You know the mayor, and he says for me
To let you in?
I know the mayor, and he says
I should show any two-bit crackpot
The door. Pat, come over here
And throw this Mr. What's-his-name
Out on the street
On his ass.

CONRAD KILMARTIN

Odd or even,
Red or black,
One to eighteen or nineteen to thirty-six:
You may as well flip a coin.
Number nine, or twenty-seven,
Or thirteen just to spite bad luck:
Your odds are better at the track.
The ball dances and rolls
And you use everything in your brain
To will it where you placed your chips,
Only to hear someone nearby declare,
"I won!" and gentlemen of leisure say,
"Congratulations,"
While I contemplate
Taking up the game
Russian-style.

MARTHA OSTRANDER

My concerts of our most cherished composer
Of the south are enhancing his popularity
In the north. My renditions of "Jeannie with the
Light Brown Hair," "Nelly Bly,"
"Old Folks at Home" and "Camptown Races"
Were so notable at the Grand Union last summer
That this season I will be singing there and
At the Clarendon.
I plan to add "Beautiful Dreamer" and
"My Old Kentucky Home" to my repertoire,
And perhaps "Why, No One To Love"
To allow my listeners to enjoy
Enriching melodies, beautifully interpreted.
My accompanist, Mr. Flynn, suggested
I conclude the programme with
"Old Black Joe."
I refused, because
Mr. Foster made a rare misjudgment
By writing a song about a poor Negro
Without the appropriate
Dialect.

KATIE WEEKS

There I was in the kitchen at Moon's on that
Summer day in 1853,
Making crullers in the pan
Like I did a thousand times before
And peeling potatoes no different
From how I do today, when a piece of the potato
Accidentally fell into the fat.
I stabbed it with a fork and set it on a plate
And George comes in, and asks, "What's this?"
He took a bite and so did I and
We both liked what we ate.
So that got George to experimenting, dropping
Thinner and thinner slices into the sizzling fat,
Letting them get dry and crispy and adding
A little salt.
In no time the rich folks and the poor folks
Started flocking to Moon's,
And I tell George it don't make no difference
To your stomach how much money you got
When it comes to the Saratoga Chip!

JIM RILEY

A swan couldn't glide across a lake more gracefully,
Or a steamboat with more command,
Than a scull propelled by deft authority.
I've rowed the waters of
Saratoga Lake since childhood,
Winning races against friends, locals
And distant challengers.
In the summer of seventy-six I was matched in a
Two mile straightway against Frank Gates,
Lathrop of Albany, Kennedy of Yale and
Charles Courtney. I pulled in front at the start,
My stroke fluid, coaxing the water for speed,
My breath in unison with my motion.
The other scullers labored and weakened as
I reached the finish in world-record time.
Dr. Hodgman has suggested
I row in England next year.
Already I envision my oars
Flowing with the slap of the waves
Toward a limitless horizon.

FLETCHER WHITCOMB

Emily comes here to drink the water,
But seldom leaves our room.
I'm out of the room all day,
And can't stomach the water.
So I read *The Times* and *The Sun* and
Socialize with leaders of industry
On the spacious veranda.
We enjoy cigars, whiskey, steak, brandy
And our own
Unassailable wealth.
This water is solely for
Women, preachers, and children
Who are genetically incapable of achieving
Manhood.

MRS. FLETCHER WHITCOMB

Fletcher and I travel to Saratoga Springs
Each summer where, if my health permits,
I partake of the waters.
In the morning I leave Congress Hall
Wearing a hat and white gloves to
Sample water from Congress Spring. After resting
In a rattan chair I venture to Hathorn,
Where the water is pungent, and again fill my glass.
By then I begin to feel faint, and
Only occasionally am I able to take a mineral bath
Before returning to our suite.
Following my afternoon repose,
I attempt to read.
The novel *Vanity Fair* brought much enjoyment
Until I encountered a quote from its author
About Saratoga: "A very dull place
For persons who are not invalids."
Mr. Thackeray, it appears, reserved his
Acute powers of observation
Strictly for his fiction.

PRISCILLA POMEROY

In the evening I lock my door,
Draw the curtains, sit at my desk
And prepare to create
Ethereal poetry.
Sun-lit golden meadows, ice-capped
Mountains, cerulean skies, bluebirds and
Robins and golden butterflies
I arrange in meter and verse
For my readings at the Clarendon.
Before retiring, I pick up
Mr. Wordsworth and ease into a night
Of radiant sleep.

CHARLES MONTGOMERY

All winter my wife, who was heavy with child,
Had cravings for coconuts. In the morning,
In the middle of the night, coconuts, coconuts!
Finding a coconut in Saratoga in the middle of March
Is like finding a rowboat in the Grand Union Hotel,
So when Dennis Alvord went to New York,
I asked him to bring back a coconut.
It was large, perfect in shape, and
My wife excitedly cracked it open,
Only to find it rotted on the inside.
In May our child was stillborn and the promised milk
Is dried and hardened.
In daylight and at night
I roam through Saratoga, observing its
Elegant hotels, splendid parks and delightful springs
And ask myself: If the whole business were bared,
How much would be diseased within?

PERRY WINDHAM

Tomorrow I leave Saratoga for the Adirondacks
Where each summer I engage an Indian guide
In the forest near Long Lake.
Each day we fish for trout and bass
And spend hours on the clear, still water,
Watching it reflect the sun,
Hearing the lark, the whippoorwill, and on the shore
The katydid. We cook our meals over an open fire,
The scent and taste of the
Blackened fish mingling with the
Smoky summer air. At night I lay in my cabin,
My guide close by, sometimes noticing
The screech of an owl or the
Rustle of a deer, or fox, outside my door.
When tempests bring rains I inhale the
Fresh sweetness, and feast on berries and nuts.

MILDRED REED

My three boys, Benjamin, James and Thomas,
All killed in the war:
Benjamin at Vicksburg, James at Gettysburg and
Thomas outside of Richmond,
Their bodies all returned to Saratoga
For burial at the Greenridge Cemetery.
My husband, John, dead two years after the war
Of a heart attack, buried beside them.
The years and years go by and I live alone
In our family home on Regent Street.
With closed eyes I see Ben running in our yard,
Chasing Jimmy, while Tom is in the cradle and their
Father is chopping wood in the back.
There's a ham to bake and a blueberry pie to be made
For dinner; I wipe my hands on my apron and
Inhale the scent of the lilac tree
Outside the kitchen door.
John comes in whistling and we look at
Tom dreaming the sweet dreams of childhood:
Lord, let their peace be mine!

MRS. ABEL A. KELLOGG

Do they still remember me, or any of my family,
In Saratoga Springs?
My father, killed when I was but a child
From complications of his fall from scaffolding
While constructing the original Congress Hall;
My mother, instilling in us all devotion to
God and respect to our fellow man;
My brothers and sisters:
Benjamin, Lewis, Rockwell, Washington, Loren
Betsey, Amelia and Nancy,
All older than me, all
Helping to raise me, all preceding me
To the grave:
Are any of their names still spoken
With reverence and esteem?
Here I pass my remaining years
In southern Illinois, recalling the
Distant springtime when I scampered
Through fields and
The streets my father drew,
And everyone called me
Phila.

GLENDA BLAINE

Have you ever inadvertently looked
At the sun or a bright candle light, then
Turn away and be left with an outline of
The object, which until it fades causes
Temporary blindness?
I never stared into a fire or the sun,
Yet the words on the page of my book
Are blurry and indistinct,
And faces of my friends no longer trigger
Recognition. Water from my eyes
Fails to clarify the vague shapes and
Odd patterns that surround me, and
Blue skies that I remember have become
Dull brown, as if
Someone attached a dirty shawl
To my eyeballs.

SLATER FINNEGAN

Sweet Jesus, comin' here from Ireland
By way of New York City
Thinkin' Johnny Logan would help me
Get a job in Saratoga,
Then Johnny and Pat Sweeney jumped off the train
In Albany while I was pickled.
Sweet Jesus, I had me a few dollars
And I got me this room on Beekman Street and
I swab the floors of the Grand Union Hotel,
Pretendin' it's the biggest poop deck in the
Irish navy.
And didn't I stare at Peggy O'Reilly
And did she eye me back and didn't the justice
Hitch us up and ain't we together now,
Drinkin' and cussin' and lovin'
Every chance we get.
And sweet Jesus, ain't Saratoga the
Prettiest place you ever did see
This side of County Roscommon!

GEORGE SHERMAN BATCHELLER

My goal was once to reflect the distinction of my life:
Harvard graduate, Lieutenant Colonel
In the Civil War, member of the
New York State Assembly and
Inspector General of the State militia,
By the grandeur of my home
Commanding Congress Park.
Its tower topped by a minaret
Augured my present role:
American Representative to
The Court of First Instance
In Cairo, Egypt.
On dusty streets I walk amid
Throngs of wayfarers with reedy arms
Protruding from tattered robes, some tramping
Without a staff, others kneeling in prayer,
Others lying prone on the ground.
I read the Koran and ponder the Laws of Islam,
And in baking heat I traverse the desert
To behold the eternal dignity of
The Great Pyramids.
Here in the company of peasants and holy men
I have named my distant home
Kasr-el-Nouzia, and consider its humble place
Beside the pyramids, the sands,
And ancient Islam.

DR. CHARLES F. DOWD

Do you know the time?
Why should the clock in Philadelphia
Be faster than New York yet
Lag behind Washington?
Why should each railroad set its own reckoning
So that the Depot Clock varies from
The watches of those living nearby?
Why should the second hand sweep past
The minute hand at the same pace in every timepiece,
Each accurate in itself, yet in discord
With each other?
Much of my time at the Temple Grove Seminary
Has been devoted to time.
Meridians are known, and
Time can become
Fixed, orderly and standard.

HENRY JAMES

At the commencement of what
I intend to be a successful career in
Letters, success being measured by the
Internal recognition that the spirit of
The word, the phrase, is conveyed in
A manner whereby the reader, possessed of his
Faculties, should not be barred from
Apprehending the thought, the idea, as
Manifested, I insist the society in which
Such labor is performed is pleasant, not
Intrusive or base, and the local surroundings
Having depreciated from those of a
Cultivated, nurturing resort to a banal town
With uncomely hotels facing each other
Like monsters, I apprehend that
Saratoga is detrimental
To refined thought, and thus I intend
To repair to Newport.

KATE TRASK

A spacious estate, and untenanted:
Broad, sloping lawns adjoining
Forests of sweet-smelling pine and hemlock
Casting shadows on limpid lakes and
Gurgling streams;
Wildflowers, ivy and vines nestled in
Ancient rocks and stones;
And the mansion, standing so handsomely
On a hill!
Memories of our visit last summer
Infuse my spirit:
Little Alan running through the trees,
His father, laughing, chasing him;
Sitting on a rock beside a slumbering pond
Inhaling the softly scented air;
Watching our shadows lengthen in a clearing;
And walking to our carriage at dusk,
Our shadows blending with the darkness
Of night.
Spencer and I are of one mind:
He will explore
Leasing the Childs Estate
In Saratoga.

WILLIAM L. STONE

What has become of the respect
The living must pay to the dead?
Our oldest burying ground, the Sadler Cemetery,
Destroyed for the establishment of building lots
Due to its benignant location off
High Rock Avenue.
How were we justified in
Disturbing the graves of our forebearers,
Denying them unending sleep?
What rationale did the Village provide
That allowed the desecration of a graveyard
Which included the remains of
The grandfather of
The President of the United States?
By failing to prevent the destruction
Of hallowed ground, we have compromised
Our own right, when our breath ultimately fails,
To infinite repose.

THEDA LIGHT

My first word was "lavender"
And I saw smiling faces in the sky
Before I recognized a cloud.
When I was five I could distinguish
Shapes and patterns around everyone
I saw.
They were amorphous, translucent,
Shimmering and veiled
All at once.
I came to know they were
Angels and by their aspect
I instinctively sensed the circumstances
Of their man, woman or child.
The doors of my home on Caroline Street
Are always open, and I've yet to
Entertain an unaccompanied guest!

ED BARROW

I am Ed Barrow, the
Handyman, helper, and jack-of-all-trades
For Theda Light.
Her friends come here each day,
And in spring and summer
I pull the hydrangeas,
Tulips and roses from the garden
For Theda to place
Throughout the house.
She says she sees angels, saying they
Pass our lifetime with us for a
Moment's amusement for themselves.
I once told Theda her angels
Were a mirage.
She responded by laughing
And told me my angel
Was forever convulsed in mirth
At the sight of me.

NOVEMBER 13, 1938

HORACE DUGGAN

Had I been born with wings instead of arms
I would have found my true purpose in life.
As a boy I'd climb to the highest branch
Of every tree
Or stand in the tower of
The Grand Union Hotel, and
People appeared more natural
The smaller they became.
When I was twenty-one, inspired by
The Spirit of St. Louis,
I earned my pilot's license.
Now I fly the most modern passenger planes
To Chicago, Baltimore, San Francisco
And everywhere in between.
When I watch the eagles and
Condors soaring higher and higher,
I see them flying in search
Of Amelia Earhart.

ROSCOE PHILLIPS

Yes, that's my rickety carriage with the
Cracked seats and peeling paint, and
Yes it's hitched to Bess,
All of twenty-four years of age,
A bit heavy and a bit slow, but if I blindfolded her
She'd still know the route from Woodlawn Avenue
To anywhere she's ever been in town.
These days the trains are noisy enough, but at least
They stay on the tracks, while
The trucks and automobiles and even
The motorcycles dart and veer and honk and weave
And would be happy running you down or
Leaving you in a ditch if you dare
Get in their way.
So Bess and I don't go out together much anymore.
And while the whippersnappers
Chase down the streets
Willy-nilly, I let Bess roam the backyard
And feed her carrots and peppermint sugar.

SAM HOCKNEY

We've lived on Woodlawn Avenue for three years,
But is seems like three hundred whenever I talk
With Roscoe Phillips.
"I saw all the great Broadway hotel fires
In the 1860s and 1870s;"
"Judge Hilton was a lout, and his
Sons were worse;"
"The gas companies would have destroyed
The mineral springs if not for Edgar Brackett."
On and on like a dull history book
He goes, and I think it makes more sense
When I hear his old nag, Bess,
Whinny and neigh.

LUELLA HOCKNEY

Sam is a carpenter and is gone all day.
I wash the clothes, change the sheets and
Fold the linens.
When he comes home at six o'clock
I have supper on the table, then he goes
To his shed with his hammer and nails and saws.
When he is late I know he's out drinking
So I leave supper for him on the stove and I
Go to bed early.
When I'm outside raking leaves sometimes
Mr. Phillips comes over.
Such a dear old man, filled with stories!
Later, when I'm lying in bed next to Sam,
I wonder if I will ever have stories to tell,
And who will be there to hear them.

GERALD WHEELER

What a time to be young in Saratoga!
Stately elms shading a grand promenade of
Prestigious men and alluring women
All along Broadway!
Gushing fountains of pure water, orchestras playing
Sublime music into the night,
Summer verdant with the fragrance of flowers, and
Banners and flags snapping in the breeze!
I married Polly in 1888.
I went to work at the bank.
We raised a son, who was killed in the war.
Polly became an invalid.
The bank dismissed me when I turned sixty.
Our savings are lost due to the depression.
The prestigious men and alluring women are gone,
Replaced by gangsters, crooks and thugs.
The sad hotels on Broadway
Mark a magnificent generation's disgust
With its descendents.

SAMUEL ROSAFF

So, business has been bad
All these years?
Hadn't noticed.
Bad business is when the
Chicago Club don't make 50 G's
On a Wednesday night
In August.
We got slots and dice and craps and
Poker and we're on the up-and-up,
See?
I run a clean house.
Go to Arrowhead or Newman's
If you want to get taken.
Don't I hand out bills from my porch
When the season ends to poor saps
Who can't beat the odds?
When I hand you a C-note,
Tell me Saratoga ain't lucky
To have Sam Rosaff as a
Part-time citizen.

EDITH ROARK

I wanted to land a career in
Vaudeville.
I ain't no cheap dance hall floozy:
I got talent and brains.
The bums in New York were suckers,
So I took up with Sammy.
His Chicago Club in Saratoga
Is a crooked dump:
He'd pay off the boys, give
Lucky his share, and we'd
Hit the whiskey.
When he passed out
I'd swipe cash from his wad.
He'd blame the boys, and
When I made nice to him
I'd get more dough.
Eventually he caught on and
In '35 I ditched him.
Want some advice?
If you see a man and a
Pack of cigarettes lyin' in the street,
Pick up the smokes.

MORTON SIMMS

I headed to Saratoga this summer when
Sid Roth gave me the inside dope on
Three horses running on three different days.
The lousy nags all finished
Up the track.
So at night I went to the Chicago Club.
My buddy Frank Short fronts the joint for
Rosaff and Luciano.
Does he fix the dice for me?
The bastard laughed when I lost and
When I went after him he
Turned his goons on me.
They broke my arm and the crooked cops
Threw me in jail for disrupting the peace.
When I got out last month
The town was empty and ugly,
Like the damned had been run out of
Hell.

JAMES A. LEARY, ESQ.

The rank-and-file, the bank teller,
The school principal, the race track bookie:
Pawns maneuvered by an
Invisible hand.
The District Attorney, Lucky Luciano,
Walter Fullerton, the Saratoga County
Republican Party: Knight, Rook, Bishop and
Queen wait at attention.
Upon authorization they begin their siege,
Confounding the adversary, surrounding the King.
Checkmate secured, they return to their stations
On the chessboard of Saratoga Springs,
Prepared to battle for a power
None of them comprehend.

VERN GUMM

No one around here believes me when I tell them
In a past life I was a counselor to Pericles,
Urging Athenian vigilance at the onset of
The Peloponnesian War.
They all laugh when I describe my life
In ancient Peru,
Mining gold and silver while my
Fellow Incans built suspension bridges and
Devised a society devoid of private property.
They walk away when I say I once
Lived in Delft, and my neighbor was
Vermeer, who had eight or nine or ten
Noisy children.
Sometimes one of them will ask,
"Vern, with everything you've done,
Why are you washing dishes at
The Grand Union?" Then I explain that
Every now and then the cosmic apparatus gets
Discombobulated.

JED KEIFFER

My father and eight other miners were
Killed in the Prospect Mine collapse in
Wilkes-Barre, Pennsylvania.
His remains showed up at our door in a pine box,
Courtesy of Prospect Mine.
Today I deliver and shovel coal into the cellars
And furnaces in Saratoga Springs, a
Blackened safeguard against winter chill.
My friends in Pennsylvania write me of the
Stirring oratory of John L. Lewis, and say
The fight for a union may be won.
My son, attending Albany College on a
Science scholarship, tells me of progress in
Heating homes by oil and natural gas.
Unions and heat via exotic sources:
May they form a human and chemical
Alliance that will leave coal
Deep in the ground.

LAURIE FIKE

I don't want it, I got no reason
To want it, I was a plain fool for letting
Jeffrey Rodgers drive me to the lake, where
He says Laurie drink some of this, and
He shoves the bottle under my nose, and
I hate the smell of gin, and he swigs down
Mouthful after mouthful, and he tries to
Jam it in my mouth, and I spit it out, and
He laughs and swigs some more, and I
Try the door handle and he yanks my arm,
And mean-like he says where you going,
And he climbs on me, and I'm flattened out,
And he rips my dress and grabs my wrists
And he pushes it in me, and I scream and
He socks my mouth, and when it's done
He drives me home and says stop crying, and
Pushes me out and drives away.
Dr. Marlowe says it'll come in April or May
But I don't want it and I've been so sick and
I don't want it at all.

DR. CARLTON WEBB

Hot water, soap and a syringe:
That's all it takes.
Oh, and seventy-five dollars
Paid in advance.
A little discomfort, yes;
An unwelcome intrusion:
Probably so;
Anxiety and loss of sleep:
That can't be helped;
Surreptitious and guarded:
If need be;
Medicine to soothe the ache:
For an extra twenty-five.
It all is done in my back office
On Congress Street
Down the block from the Jack's Harlem Club
After hours, when the secretary and
Nurse are gone.
So if you need a woman to hold your hand
Bring your sister or a friend,
And I'm not interested in how it happened,
Or what's to become of you, after
The stain is washed away.

MARY TILSDALE

For the last three months that girl has been
Doing work she had no business doing.
What could I have been thinking?
It would take her all morning to do
A tub of wash, she'd be in the bathroom
Six or seven times a day, and there were days
She'd leave early or come in late, until I was
At my wit's end.
During my visit to Dr. Marlowe last week
I brought up the matter, and as
We've known each other for forty years,
He confided to me that she is in
The family way.
Since her mother is one of those people
Who can't help, and her father being in jail,
I cannot turn my back.
If Laurie desires, she can stay with me
In one of the spare bedrooms, and when
The baby arrives, it will have a place
To call home.

FRANKLIN B. DOWD

My father refused to cower
When the ministers told him
Not to tamper with God's time;
He was not alarmed when the shopkeepers and
Jewelry store owners warned of dire consequences
For interfering with business time;
He had no fear of the rail operators who threatened
Retaliation for lost profits with the cessation of
Railroad time; and never once
Did he seek recognition
For his contributions to time.
Once on a trip west a dining car passenger
Gravely explained to him the workings of
Standard Time,
And told him to adjust his watch.
He succeeded in imposing order
Where chaos had ruled,
Yet could not avoid an ironic fate:
Returning from a call to an old friend
In the eightieth year of his life,
He was crushed to death
At the North Broadway crossing
By a train.

JIMMY SAKOWSKY

My parents thought I had an ear for music
And encouraged me to sing.
I was in chorus through High School,
But Professor Dent gave the male solos to
Peter Dunn or Ronald Bates, telling me
My voice was horribly flat.
I tried my best to pound the keys of
The family Steinway, and Professor Dent
Said I would be a fine player, if not
For my lack of rhythm, tempo and technique.
I refused to become discouraged and sought
New avenues to express my musical flair.
On Wednesday nights and sometimes on Sunday
I wow the gang at the Polish-American Club
With rousing polkas
On my concertina!

THOMAS KNOLLS

Her voice singes like a
Wayward firecracker landing and
Exploding at my feet:
"Thomas, bring my coffee!"
"Thomas, where's my purse?"
"Thomas, the sink is dripping!"
Orders, instructions and demands
Commonplace and trivial yet
Of the highest urgency
Unrelentingly assaulting my
Eardrums.
And her snoring keeps me awake
Half the night.
That's when I go to my chair
To read the funnypaper
And discover that Maggie
Still has the upper hand
On Jiggs.

MARGARET KNOLLS

The Simpsons installed a white picket fence
Around their yard, the Abernathys had
Their house painted sky blue, the Duncans
Enlarged their kitchen and added a back porch, and
What has my husband done?
I say to Madeline Abernathy, "That is such
A lovely color," and I tell Doris Simpson,
"Now you won't have to worry
About stray dogs," and
I say to Eleanor Duncan, "Your porch must be
Delightful in the summer."
And I seethe when I come home:
Peeling paint, leaking roof, the foundation
In the back beginning to sag,
And Thomas ignorant of the whole mess,
Puffing his pipe and reading his paper
In the dilapidated living room chair.

MADELINE ABERNATHY

My husband, Donald, an officer at
The Adirondack Trust Company and rector at
The Bethesda Episcopal Church; my daughter,
Joanna, on the High School Honor roll and
Soloist at the autumn concert on the clarinet;
My son, Dennis, already reading books of
Science before his tenth birthday; and
Donald's mother, Elisa, still astute at eighty-two:
Here we all live on Phila Street.
Donald is ready for breakfast at eight o'clock
In the morning and is ready for dinner at
Eight o'clock in the evening;
Elisa likes to spread her jigsaw puzzles
On the laundry room table when I'm doing the wash;
Joanna's friends traipse down to the
Basement after school where they spill apple cider
And talk about boys; when Dennis comes home
He practices on his new snare drum with his
Bedroom door wide open; and for
Thanksgiving Donald has told me his sister and
Her four children are coming, and
Please remember that
Winifred is not fond of turkey.

CONSTANCE SENGRETTI

The inclusion of my lyrical poetry
In numerous literary journals abetted my acceptance
At Yaddo.
I part the velvet curtains and open my window
To inhale the bouquet of pine, rose blossoms and
Freshly mowed grass.
Taking up my fountain pen and a sheet of
Unlined white paper, I begin:
Gondolas in Venice, sunshine warming the skin,
The far away shouts of boys chasing a ball,
A young woman, the wind brushing back her hair,
Reaching out her arms and
Kissing her lover on the mouth for the first time
Dash on my page.
A soft knock on the door, and Mrs. Ames enters.
"Don't let me disturb you.
I only wanted to drop off your lunch
So you are not hungry
In the afternoon."

EDGAR REEVES

Tomorrow my wife and I will seek
The ideal Christmas tree.
North of Caldwell I know of a grove
Where evergreens abound, and
We'll inhale the fresh scent
The moment we leave the Ford.
In a secluded spot I'll take Elizabeth's hand
And point to a tree standing tall and straight.
I'll tell her we've found
The perfect tree in the perfect spot
That no one else would have ever been able to find.
Don't you know I'll have the saw in my other hand.
And I'll use it right there, and I won't even hear the
Crackle of wood,
Or notice the juices rush from the deadened limbs.
When I'm through its shape will be
All I could hope for. I'll go back to the Ford
Where I'll have plenty of rope
To strap it on top,
Along with a shovel to bury the scraps
I leave behind.

ELIZABETH REEVES

While all of Saratoga lolls
Under its covers, my husband absently
Embarks on his nightly constitutional.
He may try to poach an egg on the
Sunroom windowsill, haul the ottoman
From the living room to the top of
The icebox, or rip pages from the
Rotogravure and try to paste them
On the hallway chandelier.
There was a recent night when in my sleep
Came the sounds of rushing water and
Him gurgling and splashing in the bath.
And it was only left for me to enter
Through the heat and steam,
Recalling the placement of the
Prescription pills, petrolatum, razor blades,
And the monogrammed terry cloth towels.

JOSIAH NANNOCK

Why doesn't Saratoga Springs honor its veterans
With an Armistice Day Parade?
Our Civil War heroes are remembered by a
Monument in Congress Park,
Our Revolutionary War battleground is
Memorialized by the battlefield nearby, while
There is no Armistice Day Parade.
High stepping brass bands! Patriotic
Anthems! Children waving flags and
Clapping their hands, all along
Broadway! Such would be a fitting tribute
To we, the veterans, marching nobly,
Victors in the war
To end all wars.

DEL HOPKINS

Getting a wife ain't that great a bargain
When you get stuck with a
Boneheaded brother-in-law.
Everything's fine so long as Abigail
Does as I say and
The kids do like I tell them,
Because the money I earn
Is plenty enough for us.
Then her brother comes and tells her their mother
Is in a bad way and needs her to come by.
So she goes over to watch her sleep in a chair
When there's ironing waiting and groceries to fetch
And when Billy and Annie get home
Their mother ain't always there.
Then at night she says she has to see her
And when I say why can't Richard go she says
He's busy and I say, busy, hell,
He don't even work, and
She says you don't understand,
You never had a brother
And I say damn right,
If there's one thing
Everybody should be
It's an only child!

DICK ROONEY

Our mother's withdrawn behavior has
Upset my sister and
Myself.
Day upon day she spends alone in our
Family home on State Street,
And at this time of year
Her reclusiveness
Worsens.
Dr. Marlowe has examined her and found
Nothing amiss, and at fifty-eight
Old age is not yet a factor.
I suppose I'll make a point of
Visiting her more often this winter,
Although my sister has more time
And should make more of an effort
Herself.

ABIGAIL HOPKINS

My father badgered mother about
Raising us, and keeping house, and
Saving money, and dressing properly,
Until the day he ran his car into a tree.
Now Richard, his favorite, hectors me
About tending her, and cooking her meals,
And reporting to him when she seems
Out-of-sorts.
And my husband hounds me about
Spending too much time with her, and
Taking care of Billy and Annie, and
Making sure his clothes are clean in the morning
So he can dirty them in the mill.
When I go there in the afternoon
The bombast of Lecture Hall is annihilated
By the sound of her sleeping breath.

FLORENCE ROONEY

On these slate-gray days of November
I wrap a woolen shawl around my shoulders
And step into the wind-swept yard.
I watch the oak and maple leaves
Swirl and fall into haphazard piles
On the dirty ground while
Squirrels scamper for nuts and tardy geese
Make their way south.
This afternoon I will light a fire,
Drink tea heavy with cream,
Swaddle myself in a blanket in my
Plush velvet chair, and
Close my eyes.

HAROLD HUMPHREY

The Book of the Lord is my companion,
The Way of the Lord is my ideal.
I travel from Argyle to Saratoga
To attend religious meetings
To counterbalance their
Nightclubs, casinos and racetrack.
To discover how the fallen spend their days,
I entered the track in August.
I heard them talking and agreeing:
Rumpleweed would prevail.
I placed my wager with a suspicious man,
Tried to see the race by
Standing on my toes, listened to them all
Hoot and yell, and didn't know what horse won
Until five minutes later.
Upon leaving I spat, remembering
The righteous will live forever
In the House of the Lord.

HENRIETTA HUMPHREY

We attend services each Sunday and
At least three other days each week.
Tea is our evening beverage and in
Summer I prepare lemonade.
Our King James Version is dog-eared
And the sanctity of our marriage is
A forgone conclusion.
So imagine my discomfit
When Harold returned from Saratoga
And immediately consulted Scripture
To determine if it is appropriate
To extract vengeance
On a horse!

FRANCES TWINING

I came to the Saratoga Spa this season
To ease the arthritis in my joints and to relieve
Headaches that had become intolerable.
On Dr. McClellan's recommendation
I sipped the Coesa and Hathorn daily,
And four times a week
I bathed in the heated waters of the
Washington Baths before returning to my rooms
In the magnificent Gideon Putnam Hotel.
In time I felt a lessening of pressure in my temples
And a limberness began to inhabit my
Arms and legs. At the end of my stay
I strolled the esplanade with
A gentleman I had met, Archer Davies,
Appreciating my newfound salubrity!

NORA JACKSON

Tell me you've walked in my shoes,
A Negro woman in a lily-white town,
Washing their clothes, baking their biscuits,
Saying, "Yes ma'am" and "Yes suh"
Twenty times a day;
My husband, Neb,
Shining their shoes, waxing their
Automobiles, shoveling their coal, and
Weeding and watering and cutting their lawns.
Tell me you could cram your man and
Three children into this ramshackle garage
On North Lane, where the heat don't always work
And the water don't always run,
Back of the high and mighty houses
Along Union Avenue.
Tell me you could feed and clothe and
Mother and nurture your own, and show them
There's hope.
Here's how it's done:
Each day when you wake, lift up your
Arms and sing in praise
Of the Risen Lord,
Thanking God Almighty for
Letting Him show the way
To the Promised Land.

INGRID LARRSEN

Fifteen cents for a loaf of bread,
Ten cents for a gallon of milk,
Shoes needed for the children,
Barely making a few dollars a day
As a seamstress when there's work
To be done, and Mr. Whitbread
Threatening to put us out if the rent
Isn't paid by Friday.
So I wrote to Aunt Josephine, and
She said she'd pay our fare if we
Want to come home and
Stay with her and Uncle Lars
Until I find a place of our own.
And I told Greta and Sven
That taking a trip on a boat
Will be a wonderful adventure, and
They will learn to ice skate,
And the winters will be much prettier
In Stockholm than they ever were
In Saratoga Springs.

NATHANIEL WHITBREAD

The Swedish woman living over the garage
Can't seem to come up with the rent.
The Negro woman who cleans
Tuesdays and Thursdays says she's
Going back to Georgia unless
I pay her fifty cents more a week.
The Italian at the filling station
Doesn't have time to check the oil in my Buick,
Or see if the tires are properly inflated.
Don't you see it's all part of a
Disturbing pattern?
The United States cannot be mentioned
Without the word "depression," and as a solution
Washington taxes the businessman
To ensure that those who barely work at all
Are provided for.
Once they start getting money
On the dole, the citizenry
Commits itself to sloth!

DAVE BADER

Hiking Tongue Mountain with Bill Rosenblatt,
Talking of climbing the High Peaks,
Slaloming in Vermont and
Snowshoeing this winter near Lake Placid,
I never saw the rattler
Sunning itself on the trail.
My foot missed it by an inch
When all at once it rattled and coiled and
Stuck its fangs in my calf and held on until
Bill beat it off with a stick.
We scrambled down the mountain, and
By the time we got to the hospital
It was too late to save my leg
Below the knee.
Now you won't see me hiking Tongue Mountain,
Climbing the High Peaks or
Snowshoeing near Lake Placid!

IRENE SUTHERLAND

My husband and I departed Saratoga Springs
Via carriage following our marriage in 1898,
And we returned for the first time last week
For the funeral of my aunt.
Woodlawn, that grand estate, in shambles,
Congress Hall razed, the other hotels
Desperately in need of paint and maintenance and
Boarded up for winter, and
The prevalence of distressing gambling halls
Assailed and offended my senses.
Aunt Sophia was my final remaining relative here,
And tomorrow Gregory and I will return to Flint,
Where he is a top executive
In the automobile industry.
We travel in a 1939 Oldsmobile sedan, and
I won't look back as its exhaust
Merges with the grimy dust.

CAROLYN WALLIS

I'd worked at Van Raalte Knitting for sixteen years
When I began to feel drowsy every afternoon.
When I came home I'd tell Herman I was tired
And went to bed early, yet found myself
Needing more rest in the morning, and
Coffee four or five times a day didn't help.
Dr. Marlowe prescribed little coated pills and
Told me I needed to keep my mind active
To stay awake. I started nodding off during
Lunch breaks and wouldn't get back to work
On time, and then Mr. Spooner told me they needed
Someone more reliable, and let me go.
Now I stay home and try to complete my housework
Before the next bout of sleep, and
Herman asks himself out loud
How he could have ever married someone
So depressingly lazy.

HERMAN WALLIS

I work with my brothers at the
Finch-Pruyn Paper Mill in Glens Falls.
I drive to work,
Stay on my feet all day,
Drive home, and stay
Wide awake all the time.
And here's Carolyn
Plopped in a chair and
Constantly falling asleep
In the middle of the day.
But I bite my tongue and
Keep my temper.
My brothers introduced me to Anita Lawson
And I've been stopping at her place lately.
I'm looking for a lawyer
Who specializes in divorce.
The way I see it (and my brothers agree)
It's a clear-cut case:
If I have no companionship,
I have a legal right
To get it
Someplace else.

EVANGELINE RUHLE

I was fanning myself in the rocker on
June 24, 1894, with Tabitha, three months old,
Sleeping beside me in the bassinet,
When I closed my eyes for a fateful moment
In the sweltry heat.
Henry came home from the Hotel, the
Slam of the door jolting me awake, and there was
Tabitha, face down, not breathing.
I screamed, Henry pushed and pushed on her chest,
And finally those tiny lungs,
Going so long without air,
Began to heave.
Years of doctors did no good; Henry blamed me and
Eventually moved into the Hotel, taking Tabitha.
When Henry died she came home.
Now Tabitha sleeps soundly, and every morning
She awakes with the conviction that past wrongs
Have been corrected, and tells me
She's ready to play
In the Kensington Hotel.

JACK PORT

This damn town is too much for anybody,
Those damn hotels on Broadway rot and
Take up space ten months of the year
When no one's there.
In summer, they gamble at Riley's,
And Piping Rock, and Arrowhead,
And when the track is open that's
Where they go, thinking they can
Make a million
Betting on a horse's ass
While the best job I can get is
Cleaning up the shit they leave behind.
There have been fires here before
And one day when they're busy being stupid
I'll start another and the United States will become
Cheap kindling wood.
When they search for the arsonist
I won't be found,
So the idiots will blame the Second Coming
Of Mrs. O'Leary's cow.

JUDGE ERNEST HOP

McReynolds, VanDevanter, Sutherland, Butler
Aligned with Hughes or Roberts: corporation lawyers
Intent on dismantling laws for the people
In the interest of business avarice.
Joe Robinson found dead in the swelter of
Acrimonious debate, dashing the prospect of
New blood supplanting decrepit conceits.
As Abraham Lincoln rose from humble soil
To bind the wounds of a divided nation,
Now from the ignoble sect of white hoods and
Robes appears justice elevated and invigorated.
Their disreputable authority muted,
The Four Horsemen recede and
A government of beneficence
Acquires constitutional muster, guided and goaded
By justice ironically christened
Black.

EUGENIA PENROSE

My home on Madison Avenue
Is one of the finest in Saratoga.
The mahogany banister shines,
All five fireplaces are ablaze in winter
And I never step in the kitchen.
I'm friends with the Pitneys and
At the track I sit
In the Whitneys' private box.
My caretaker oversees a staff of seven,
And if any of them are caught drinking,
They are dismissed.
In winter, I travel to Miami by train
And marvel that the colored help
Can keep their jobs because they move
So slowly.
Society would be enhanced
If the working classes became invisible
And still performed their tasks.

JULIA CALLAHAN

I would stand for hours with my girlfriends
On the corner of East Congress Street and Putnam
In front of Mr. Morrisey's Saratoga Club
And wait for him to come by.
From his pockets he'd pull out taffy, licorice
And sometimes dollar bills which we would spend
In the Arcade.
Years later my children would watch
Mr. Canfield supervise the planting of the
Italian Gardens and in the afternoon
He would sometimes take them through
The building where the rich men gambled.
Last week I told my grandson the story of how
One day in the 1870s Mr. Morrisey donated the
Entire day's proceeds at the track to commence the
Fund to erect old School 7.
Then yesterday when I had the ladies over for tea,
Eugenia Penrose saw Mr. Morrisey's picture
In my scrapbook and asked,
"Who was he?"

JOHNNY McKEE

My colt spent the winter of 1930 in
Agua Caliente, then Tanforam in the spring,
Not racing much and not winning much.
We shipped him east on the Californian
And when we reached Saratoga he lifted his ears,
As if he remembered winning there in the slop
In the 1929 Grand Union.
When it poured down rain the night before,
I knew the Travers was ours.
And they all bet on Gallant Fox, with Sande,
Or Whichone, with Sonny, and those two
Dueled for the lead, Sonny trying to push
Sande away from the rail, and my colt
Shot through an opening big enough for a
Caravan, and thirty thousand people saw,
And millions more heard or read about my
One hundred to one long shot,
Winning by open lengths!

FRITZ BELLAMY

Why at Saratoga do they talk and talk
About that miserable Travers of 1930?
That year belonged to the Fox, winning
The Derby, the Preakness, the Belmont Stakes,
And I bet more and more on him each race,
Believing him unbeatable.
At Saratoga the only other horse with a chance was
Whichone, and knowing the Fox would not bend
If they went eye to eye, I was set
To nab a bundle.
So Sande sent the Fox right out of the gate,
And Sonny Workman made Whichone dig in
When he should have laid off, and sure enough
Whichone was done in the stretch, but that horse
No one in his right mind could have bet
Splashed past everyone.
After the race Sande and Workman scuffled,
And Whichone never raced again,
And every year when I go to Saratoga
Somebody tells me how he beat the odds
And made a fortune on
Jim Dandy.

ANASTASIA POLLARD

I starred as Isabella in the High School
Production of *Measure for Measure*
Opposite Rex Pollard as Claudio.
Didn't he proposition me before
We left High School, and didn't we
Marry two years later, and didn't he
Take up with Loren Tate before our
Third Anniversary, and run away with her
To Boston?
Now I read *Hamlet*, *Othello* and
King Lear, and find myself pondering
Mankind's capacity for forgiveness,
And revenge.

BARNARD FLEMMING

Huck Finn and I
Floated down the Mississippi,
Watching Leopold Bloom
Wander the shore where
J. Alfred Prufrock
Ate a peach.
We were sailing into a
Lustrous sunset when
Jay Gatsby churned by
In a gilded raft, pursued in a rowboat
By Jason Compson.
Then mother hammered on the door,
"Wake up, Barnard, dinner's ready!"
And father barged in and
Hustled me downstairs, where
Pot roast, peas and milk awaited.
The river rushed on when I got back,
And I decided I didn't have it so bad
Compared to
Akaky Akakievich!

FRANK SULLIVAN

When the Queen Dowager of American tracks
Celebrated her 30th birthday
An individual who later became
A correspondent of minor repute came along,
And this person knows there's no proven formula
For keeping the old girl down.
This youngster began as water boy at the pump
In the old betting ring, nervously carrying drinks
To Lillian Russell.
Later, he took to wearing long pants
And worked in the press box, and although
He went on to write for various publications
In a southern metropolis, he has never
Lived more than two blocks away.
Today this correspondent spends whatever time
He can at the track during its annual summer gala,
Until the hour when he and his mates
Gather for a final round the Worden.
And if he exceeds his limit, it's no trouble
To switch to a bottle of
Saratoga Geyser the following day!

MONTE WOOLLEY

Stand aside, scoundrel,
Witness my stellar performance!
Suave and gallant, I kneel before my betrothed:
"Darling, my heart beats in rapture
When you're near."
Rugged and athletic, I race with the ball:
"Out of my way, blackguards,
Out of my way!"
Captaining the ship on the roiling sea,
The pirate vessel looms:
"Fie, villains! Set your sights, mates!"
Zounds, man! Buy me a scotch and soda
At the Worden, and I'll give you an education
In drama.

FREDERICK OARE

Had they been spending their evening
Listening to the immortal rhapsodies of
Brahms, the haunting melancholy of
Tchaikovsky, or the stirring drumbeat
Of Wagner, they never would have known of
Aliens in Grover's Mill.
The interlopers caught
The townspeople unawares and
Would stop at nothing short of
Annihilation.
The citizens screamed, fled and
Died, and they all began sweating and
Shaking, straining to
Make sense of the mayhem through the
Static of their radios.
Their civilization buckled and swayed
Until the unexpected moment of
Revelation, as if
They'd spent their evening
Listening to Beethoven's Ninth.

SADIE CHRISTOPHER

You know best what's best for you:
A motto naturally learned and felt yet
Seldom enacted.
Pressures, commitments, obligations:
You should do this and you should do that,
Mind and heart in conflict with
Authenticity.
My confidants in Saratoga:
Do you live in harmony with your own
Individualized nature?
Do you stride down Broadway
Unfettered, autonomous and sovereign?
Or are complaints, grievances,
Negotiation and compromise the
Coordinates of your life?
Knowledge is grand,
Feeling sublime:
Without equivocation, can you complete
The trinity?

WILMA TAYLOR

I feel sorry for him,
Raising his boy with the help of his sister
After his wife walked out.
She was too good for him, too good for everybody,
Wearing pearls and gaudy makeup
While the rest of us
Struggle to make a few dollars in a town
Half-dead most of the year.
Saratoga is better off without the high and mighty,
Always has been, if only they didn't
Ruin things before they left.
Poor man!
Tomorrow I might bake a cake and bring it over;
I'm sure Luke likes chocolate as much
As any other boy, and it will do them both good
To know that their neighbors
Are there to help.

KRISTOV KOSOLOWSKY

It's makin' me nervous and sick when
I think about it, and I'm thinkin' about it
All the time.
My cousins and nieces and nephews
Livin' in Poland, and they don't know if
They can come here because
Everyone in Poland wants to come
To America because of what's happenin'
Over there.
And sometimes when I'm on the street
Or in the store and I start talkin' about it,
Most everyone seems to say,
It ain't really so bad over there, people in
Those countries should know how to
Take care of themselves.
So I say to them, don't you think
If the United States had Russia
On the left, and Germany on the right,
That we'd go to war on them before they'd
Do the same to us?

PERTH CONBOY

A city grows and prospers
By discarding the old and derelict
To make way for the new.
From the window of the Athenaeum
Above the Colonial Restaurant
Observe the Grand Union Hotel:
Elephantine, gargantuan, rotting,
Unwelcoming and empty.
Just as the dentist removes
The abscessed tooth to prevent
The spread of contagion,
We must raze the Grand Union.
I would then be happy to serve
On a consortium
To determine how the land
Could best be used
For the enrichment of
Saratoga Springs.

MARILYN CONBOY

My husband believes he speaks of
The human condition in terms
Significant and compelling.
Yet instead of addressing the unraveling of
Europe, research in medicinal cures,
Norman Thomas and the drive for
Organized labor, or at least advancements
In the motor car, he scouts Saratoga
To reach a conclusion no more profound than,
"The old must go to make room for the new."
So the Grand Union rots,
Woodlawn crumbles, the casinos become
More tawdry,
And each morning before he delivers his first
Pronouncement, I watch him adjust his
Pince-nez and comb his white goatee.

JANEY ABERCALM

My father, who worked in the stables
Behind the Hoyt property,
Drank whiskey and rum every weekend and
Hit my mother until she blacked out.
She got away by hanging herself from the beam
Above the kitchen table.
My father kept drinking until they
Took him away, and
I went on to live in many homes
And have entertained many people
Wearing starched white shirts
And clean jackets.
I very much enjoy the juices they bring,
Although the tablets don't always taste
Like candy, and when I wake up
In the morning I sometimes sense
I've had uninvited visitors
Overnight.

CATHERINE EPS

I never entertained a gentleman caller until
Tommy Palmer gained
My mother's permission in my
Senior year. We'd visit Saturday nights,
Although I had to retire by ten o'clock
To get ready for church Sunday morning.
When Tommy kissed me on the cheek I didn't resist,
But when he tried to become too familiar I told him
To stop. The catechism warns of
Severe consequences for such behavior
Before marriage.
I'm forever thinking of what might have happened,
And when I'm at Mass I say
An extra Act of Contrition
For Tommy.

NABELLA EPS

I've instructed my daughter to obey and fear the Lord
Since she was a child.
I would stand at her door to make sure she said
Her Hail Marys and Our Fathers before bed,
And grace before meals is compulsory.
Taking the name of our savior in vain
Is grounds for punishment, and lipstick,
Makeup and gaudy attire are forbidden.
And to those who question the effectiveness
Of devout faith, look at Catherine!
Humble and pious in the sight of the Lord, and
Planning to attend Mass tomorrow to mark
Her forty-second birthday.

BUDDY HALL

Hot dog! Tim Gorman bet me
Fifty cents Mary Beth Suter would
Turn me down when I asked if she'd
Go with me to the school dance.
He was with me when I asked and
When she said, "Sure, Buddy,"
I socked him on the shoulder
And later I said, "I told you,
She likes me!"
So Tim said he thinks
Barbara Wilcox likes him and
I said, "Go ahead and ask her and
Keep your fifty cents."
So after the dance maybe
The four of us will go to
Helprin's Pharmacy for a
Root beer float or maybe
It'll just be Mary Beth
And me!

SALLY YOUNG

Mr. Keeps and M.K. Jones and Ambassador Blue
Sleep with me each night.
Sometimes Mr. Keeps falls out of bed
Because M.K. Jones is a big dog and takes up
Lots of space.
After midnight, Ambassador Blue
Likes to go downstairs for cookies and cake
When there's some in the kitchen.
He shares the cake with M.K. Jones
While Mr. Keeps stares out the window
At the stars.
Ambassador Blue became an ambassador because
He can speak Chinese and do arithmetic tables
In his head. When the sun comes up, M.K. Jones
Has a tummy ache, and Mr. Keeps
Is lying on the floor, and crying,
Because the stars are gone.

KEITH GUEST

I needed to know that blonde who works
At the cash register at Woolworth's
So I'd buy socks and pens and
Goldfish bowls and I pretended I didn't notice
Her eyes when she told me she was Dolores Dell.
When she'd bite her lip and twirl her hair over her ear
And look down and look back up at me and smile
I couldn't wait any more and asked her
To have a tuna fish sandwich with me
At Woolworth's lunch counter.
She said she lives with her parents and went to work
After High School but that was two years ago and
She's learned a lot about people since then and
Her parents are nice enough only
They don't seem interested
In everything that's happening inside her soul.
And she said I must meet
All sorts of interesting people selling
Newspaper ads for *The Saratogian* and
I looked at her and said I sure do.
So I asked her if she'd go on a date with me
Next Saturday night and she said she would
And if I think about anything except the way
She twirls her hair between now and then
It would be a miracle.

DOLORES DELL

When I go out on dates, sometimes I get tired of
Listening to them.
Bobby Thompson is always talking about
Playing center field for the Geysers because he's
The team's fastest player; Bruce Dowling talks about
Going to college even though he's
Already twenty-five; George Morse is
Friendly enough, but his glasses are so
Thick that his eyes look funny and
It's hard to concentrate on what he's saying.
Now, that salesman from the newspaper
Wants to take me out Saturday and I said yes
Even though he seems to talk
More than the others combined.
Oh, well, at least he's handsome when he wears
His suits and his fedora, and he comes from
Buffalo, and I've always said if there's
One place I'd like to learn more about and
Maybe visit someday it's
Niagara Falls.

VALINDA FEATHERS

The Bowers boys call me a bowling ball,
I tilt from side to side when I walk
And the last time I tried bending my knees
I fell, giving Pat Edwards
A vexing job getting me up again.
Mrs. Larrsen, the seamstress, alters my dresses
And my special bed is
Square in shape and low to the ground
To prevent accidents.
Diets and exercise and treatments don't work,
And Dr. Marlowe says
Nothing can be done.
So I live with my parents and sit in my chair
Facing Circular Street where each day
I watch the children to go back and forth to school,
Ready to smile and wave in case they happen
To look in the window.

TIM GORMAN

She's so fat I don't know how they can squeeze her
Into her chair. How much does a person have to eat
To get that fat? Billy Duffy didn't believe me when
I told him how fat she is, so I told him
To walk past her house after school.
She's always sitting there in the window,
And after he walked by last Wednesday he told me
She was just sitting there, fatter than fat,
Waving at all the kids walking by.
Some of the little kids and the girls
Don't know any better so they wave back, like
It's something I want someone seeing me doing,
Waving to someone who is so fat
They must need a crowbar to get her out of her chair.
Billy said, "I bet she smells too," and I said,
"How much food do you think she eats?'
And Billy said, "She probably eats lard all day."
I can't wait until it snows because then
When I walk by I'm going to throw snowballs
At her window and then maybe she'll find
Someplace else in her house to sit so
I don't have to walk by her house every day
And have to look
At how fat she is.

VICTOR McGRATH

How I hated Saratoga and all its vices
After the murder of my son, found in a ditch behind
The Chicago Club with
Two bullets in his chest!
Tongues wagged of the killing for weeks,
John's dealings with Lucky Luciano
Became the stuff of brazen gossip, and the papers
Couldn't stop giving me calls: was it true his debts
Ran into the thousands of dollars, and was it true
That time and again I bailed him out?
In venomous rage I drove one night on
Circular Street and somehow didn't see
The huge form of Valinda Feathers
Before I struck her.
When they took her to the hospital she was told
Her weight had cushioned the blow, and
She and her family refused to
Press charges against me,
Saying my suffering was more profound
Than theirs.
From the folds of her enormous body
She looked up at me and smiled, and
My anguished cries were
Absorbed and honored
When they should have drawn nothing but
Contempt.

JOE STOKES

I worked for Luciano,
Rothstein and Schultz,
Rubbing out McGrath
In Saratoga, then
Beardsley in New York.
I took my cut and
Kept quiet but now
Luciano thinks I know
Too much and Sawyer
Came for me last night and
I just got away down the
Fire escape.
I'm getting out of New York
Headed to hell-knows-where
On three hundred bucks
And if my nerves and
Stomach kill me it'll be
Better than having it done
By a bullet
In the brain.

LUCILLE QUINN

First they're brats and then
They're bullies:
Stealing lollipops and pulling ribbons
From the little girls' hair;
Talking and shouting with vulgar words;
Jabbing and poking and hitting each other
When there's no one else to punch.
When we leave school they go
To that lady's house on Circular Street,
Just waiting for her
To look out the window
So they can point and laugh.
They were there again Friday when
The older boy who lives next door
Told them to scram and they all ran quick
When he started after them.
I told Ellie how mean they were
And she said she was glad he
Chased them away and we both said
We wished the other boys would be more like
Harrison Melrose.

FATHER PAUL McGREGOR

Bless me father for I have sinned
They all say upon entering the confessional, and
According to my vows I believe
Each craves absolution.
The man whose son was murdered by gangsters
Seeks forgiveness for anything he had done
To cause his son to go astray; the woman
Deformed from birth begs God's pardon for
Occasionally blaming Him for her troubles;
The old man cries in remorse for the times
He cursed the Lord for allowing him to
Live so long with his wife and daughter in the grave;
The young woman begs for guidance in the
Raising of her child, yet to be born,
Without a father.
Their supplications echo through the silent church
As I walk to the Altar to observe a form,
Illuminated by flickering candle light,
In the throes of death.

LUCY SWINBOURNE

Furrows already appearing on her brow;
Fingertips of her right hand gently touching
Her face beside her lip; her checkered blouse and
Rumpled jacket open in the front, nearly exposing
Part of a breast; her eyes searching
Beyond her tent in the camp in the
Nipomo Valley.
On her left shoulder a girl facing away,
Her little hand covering her unseen face;
Another child's head
Nestled on her right shoulder,
Perhaps sleeping, perhaps wishing
The lady with the camera would finish.
Then they could leave the tent,
And see if the sun had melted the frost
So the vegetables would not be frozen
In the fields.

H.B. SETTLE

Camera in hand, I have walked the streets of Saratoga
For the entire century, photographing
Hotels, homes, the Masons, the Elks,
Congress Park, casinos, children riding bicycles,
Thoroughbreds, and people I never knew
As they appeared before my lens.
My studio on Putnam Street is home to dozens of
Photographers coming here in the summer who sign
Their name on the wall. One of them,
Lucy Swinbourne, has collected from magazines
The photographs of Dorothea Lange, at work for the
Farm Security Administration.
Etched and lined faces, the gesture of a hand,
The play of light on a woman's dress,
Or a child's hair,
Generate instant apprehension of
Lives filled with pain, anguish, torment, and
Hope.
From dusty boxes I remove
The Parker family reunion of 1913,
The dinner honoring George Foster Peabody,
Bertrand Chester at the track and
The Markle wedding at Yaddo, and puzzle over
Their mysteries.

MAY 7, 2005

JENNIFER MILLAY

Flowers in bloom! Scents of spring!
Emma bounds from her room,
"Mama, I'm awake, let's go outside!"
Down the steps, running into the
Emerald yard on the sun-splashed day
Emma sees Jill Bant open her downstairs door,
"There's Jill!" "Hello, doll face,"
Jill smiles and sips her coffee.
"Bye," says Emma, and we stroll
The busy, shiny, shady streets, smelling the
Dew-flecked grass, breathing the sweet spring air.
At the Farmers' Market we buy fresh strawberries,
"Let's get some, they're yummy,"
Roses and geraniums.
"Here's a cookie, Emma," and she munches it
All the way to Congress Park where she
Chases the ducks. "Mama, if I catch a duck,
Can I keep it?" Past the carousel with its
Gleaming horses, "In a few weeks, Emma,
You can go for a ride," past the houses with
Bright colors and people waving from porches,
We ramble home.
Jill Bant looks up from her magazine,
"Emma, your flowers are beautiful!"
"Mama, bend over," Emma whispers in my ear,
"I want to give Jill the yellow flower,
And I want you to keep the red ones."

HARRISON MELROSE

For sixty years I've opened my eyes
To see Lucille. Today she hands me my cane
And gently guides me down the stairs.
Our daughter Anne and her husband
Are making pancakes which are
Easy for me to chew.
I sit in the cushioned chair at the kitchen table and
Lucille adjusts my oxygen tank.
Our granddaughter Sara, home from college,
Sneaks up from behind and kisses me
On the back of my neck.
The phone rings and our son Lewis says
He'll stop by later to cut the lawn,
If we don't mind one more for dinner.
Sara spreads butter on my pancakes,
Anne pours my orange juice,
Lucille hands me a fork,
And I look at a family
That through a power greater than
Any I could ever summon,
Came to be mine.

JONDA WILEY

The closest lake is Lake Lonely, but
They built a golf course there and having
Fat men in plaid pants close by won't do.
The closest river is the Hudson, only
I might be seen going through Schuylerville and
Boats and ships still go between
Canada and New York.
Then there's Saratoga Lake where people
All along the shore have rafts and canoes and
They're always puttering about.
There are lakes and streams in the
Adirondacks which you need a map to find,
And that takes away the point.
So the answer is the ocean,
Only a day away, where the air
Smells like salt and
The only appropriate measurement
Is fathoms.

CY GILLESPIE

Tap, tap, tap on the barometer,
A peek out the window and flick,
On goes the Weather Channel.
High-pressure all day long!
Mack Pope, hustle over to Clancy's
For that eye-opener.
Cirrus clouds with the dew point dropping.
Jeffrey Foster, pot some
Martha Washingtons for the Farmers' Market.
What's that over the Midwest?
A front near Kentucky?
By gosh, Bing O'Flaherty, I hope it won't rain
At Churchill.
Tap, tap, tap, it's still going up!
Look out the window and there it is!
Blue skies and green leaves and crisp air
And Saratoga sitting smack dab in the middle
Of pitch-perfect weather.

JACK McANALLY

I know all about workout patterns,
Drop downs, pace figures, early speed,
Blinkers on, turf to dirt, weight allowances,
Cold jockeys, hot barns, horses for the course,
And trainers who win with
First time starters.
I play pick-threes, the pick-four,
The pick-six, parlays, exactas, trifectas, and
If the odds are right, horses to win.
I bet two, three, sometimes
Four grand a day, keying my
Top selections, laying low on
Non-betable races.
So how is it that I eked out a profit
Of two hundred bucks at Saratoga last summer,
After being up ten thousand after three weeks?
And how is it that Ryan Brewster,
Who'd never been to the track, won
Thirty thousand on
A single pick-six ticket?
Bullshit!

RYAN BREWSTER

Jack McAnally refused to speak to me
After we went to the track and I won
Thirty seven thousand, four hundred eleven dollars
On the pick-six.
When I got home with my winnings
My wife's kisses were longer than a race, and
Last month she took a leave of absence
From her job, and in June we're expecting
Our first child, Elizabeth Joanne.
Jack McAnally thought it was dumb luck
That made me rich, so I didn't tell him
My system: I played the last six numbers
On my Social Security Card!

PAMELA CAMINO-ABDUL

My husband and I work as researchers at
The Albany Medical Center and
We purchased a home
On the outskirts of Saratoga Springs.
We lived near the golf course and the people
Across the street were disappointed
When they learned we don't golf.
Our next door neighbors drove SUVs and asked
When we planned on trading in our
1997 Beretta.
One day we received a note in our mailbox,
Asking, if it is not too much trouble,
To please water our lawn and
Perhaps purchase some fertilizer if we
Didn't plan on planting any trees.
We stayed in that house for eighteen months.
Now we live in Albany where
Our neighbors are Mohammed Al Sinor,
Neville Wilkins, Jackie Grabowski and
Katherine Smith.

AUGUSTON BLANCHARD

My father bought four lots on
Ludlow Street in 1961,
When Saratoga Springs was chock-full of
Boarded up houses and ramshackle shacks,
And a Real Estate Empire began.
While 19th century buildings were wrecked and
Neighborhoods obliterated under the auspices of
Urban Renewal, he purchased property dirt-cheap
On White Street, Fifth Avenue, and finally
North Broadway.
Our family leased, sold and built,
Property values skyrocketed, and
We earned for ourselves
Enormous profit.
Today we're pillars of the community:
Running the Real Estate business,
Raising rents when necessary,
And ensuring that Saratoga Springs welcomes
The right kind of people.

MAJOR GERALDINE TRUMAN

Last November the Salvation Army
Requested permission to place our
Christmas Kettle in front of Blanchard Realty
In the Collamer Building.
Our phone calls were not returned,
Our letters were not answered, and finally one day
I made an appointment to meet with
Auguston Blanchard.
Didn't I realize he didn't want any ringing bells
Outside his office, and didn't I know we take up
Too much space on Broadway, and why was the
Salvation Army logo so similar in design to the
Blanchard Realty sign, and what was I doing
Talking to him anyway, when he had
Legitimate clients to meet?
We located in front of the
Adirondack Trust Company instead, and the
Bank president has never once walked by
Without depositing at least a dollar in the kettle.

JONATHAN CLAY, ESQ.

I practiced law in the Collamer Building
From my admittance to the Bar until last year.
My lease expired, and Auguston Blanchard
Doubled my rent, citing increased taxes
And maintenance expenses.
Of course he wanted me gone:
I represent the indigent, and work for
Legal Aid, and belong to the
Green Party.
Now I practice from my home on
Clinton Street and appear before the bench
For those accused of assault, harassment,
Probation violations and DWI.
After the hearing, trial and verdict
I watch most of my clients
Get hauled off to jail,
Sentenced by judges who through
Sheer determination usually manage to
Stifle their yawns.

ANNA CATHERINE TIVERS

The Library Guild
Succeeded magnificently in the Fund Drive
For computer improvements in the Childrens' Room
And to celebrate we held a picnic at the
Saratoga Golf and Polo Club.
We strung out a piñata filled with toys
And let the children take turns whacking it
After everyone finished their ice cream.
Child after child softened it until
Jackie Clay let loose a huge swing
And the piñata split, spilling its loot.
We all scrambled for the knickknacks and
While bending over to pick up a toy mouse
I was shoved from behind and fell headfirst
In the grass.
When I stopped feeling woozy
The Treasure Hunt was over, and Madge Burke
Told me I'd been flattened
By Auguston Blanchard, who was hell-bent to snatch
A Tonka Truck!

CHARLOTTE RAWLINGS

Sure, that busybody Madge Burke fingered
Auguston Blanchard for leveling
Anna Catherine Tivers
At the Treasure Hunt.
In March, Blanchard Realty sacked
Madge's husband Wendell for
Trying to let Jonathan Clay
Submit a late bid on the Bragg property
After Cynthia Lowe fired Madge
At Rosen & Leventhal
For gossiping more than working,
And Clay's suit for her back wages failed.
So Madge and Clay aim their bull's eye on
Auguston Blanchard.
And, at the Treasure Hunt, I barely nudged
Anna Catherine when I reached
For the macadamia nuts.

HAZEL DeSOTO

The Friends of Congress Park, of which I was
Co-founder, did all we could to prevent
The desecration of our treasured jewel.
We solicited funds from caring members
Of the community, we engaged competent counsel,
We stated our case clearly and forthrightly, and
Our petition was thrown out in Court.
The interpretation of the law was that the
City had a right to build it across from Putnam Street,
Within easy sight of Spit and Spat and
The Spirit of Life.
Since it opened I have
Excused myself from Park activities,
And when I drive by I avert my eyes.
Isn't it a shame: Saratoga has come so far,
And now we must endure
The honky-tonk!

ALICE DeSOTO

So I lugged out my antique books
And sepia photographs and brittle articles
On parchment paper to show my sister how
Putnam Street once crossed Spring precisely
Where the carousel is today, before it met
East Congress at Morrissey's Casino;
And how one-hundred years ago
Congress Hall spread across Broadway
And would have engulfed the Arts Center and
The Spirit of Life that stand there now; and how
Clark's bottling works had operated
Around the clock across from
Congress Spring; and how
Richard Canfield's Italian Gardens and
Sculpture completely surrounded
Spit and Spat, and that whole block
Wasn't even a part of the original
Congress Park!
And don't you know she shoves my
Papers aside, and moans and crabs
About the desecration of a purely subjective
History.

GRETA GOLDING

They gave me such an easy job to start my
Career at Blanchard Realty: renew the lease
For the DeSoto dames on Union Avenue.
Mailing it wouldn't do, might I call on them
Personally?
Hazel (or was it Alice?) poured my tea and
Fretted about the rotting hemlock in the yard;
Alice (or was it Hazel?) sliced my cake and
Told me stories about someone named
Trask and about the pigeons
Roosting in the chimney;
Alice and then Hazel, or Hazel and then Alice
Asked if I had a husband, and where I went
To school, and how long have I lived
In Saratoga, and even though it's been oiled
The pantry door still creaks, and please
Stop by again because the kettle is always on.
Whew!
Anyway, the old gals signed the lease
And at the office they told me
Auguston Blanchard hadn't raised their rent
In fifteen years!

VITAS ALEXSIS

This summer my eight-year old boy and I
Will travel to Saratoga Springs to find
A sliver of our past.
On back roads winding past farms and
Through mountains Eric will play with his
Game boy, listen to music,
Fall asleep, or ask me again
The reason for our journey.
While he reads comic books or
Gazes out the window he may hear me expound
On wood molded and carved,
Pistons and gears, circular motion,
And calliopes.
In Saratoga Springs our goal will emerge
When we see children and adults
Riding polished and gleaming horses.
And if he chooses, Eric will join them, and go
Round and round on a horse
Crafted by his great-great-grandfather,
Marcus Illiuns.

GREGORY WESTON

He was my wife's brother, and lived with us
Until his death at seventy-three.
He'd step from the curb and march beside
Lawrence Crane and the Chief of Police in the
Flag Day Parade; he'd barge into
A different classroom every day at
Lake Avenue School and
Try to guess childrens' names;
Or he'd walk around town talking out loud to himself
Until Theresa or I would bring him home.
Twice a week he'd go to Pappy's barbershop.
Pappy would set down his scissors,
Put a quarter in one hand
And a nickel in the other, saying,
"Now, Bill, take your time before you choose."
He'd take the nickel and trudge off mumbling
While Pappy and the men laughed
Beneath their crew cuts.
Once I asked him which coin was worth more
And he said, "not the nickel,"
So I asked why he always took it.
"Because if I took the quarter,
They wouldn't play the game."

PINSLEY CRUPP, ESQ.

First that day it was opposition to lift stay
Filed by Nescor & Newly on behalf of
Conseco Mortgage against Baines.
After that, reviews of notices of claims filed
Of Cuddup, Ralfstein and Pierce.
Two new clients came next,
Tessier and Yates,
Neither of whom was retained.
I had meant to do the order to show cause
On Murphy that afternoon to save his Cadillac,
But I let it go.
I went on vacation the next day, and
Two months later I received
A notice from the Commission.
Murphy had filed a complaint,
Alleging unprofessional representation.
The next thing I knew, they started poking into
My escrow accounts and discovered
My draw so I could keep up
On my mortgage payments.
I let the foreclosure proceed and
Roomed for four months
With a former bankruptcy client
In the Saratoga County Jail.

GINGER POOLE

With my long delicate fingers I learned
My special skill: wiggle a finger and
There's a rooster! Cup my hands downward, a man
With a beard! A sly turn of the wrist,
A cat on a blanket! And in a flash, a
Giraffe walking along!
But the image formed on the retina is
Turned upside down, negatives are
Reversed from the picture that's taken and the
Photograph that's developed, and a smile on
Your face can mean happiness, or ecstasy, or
Tolerance, or contentment, or nothing
At all. I watch for profiles, contours and
Silhouettes, and the image is crystallized
When the switch is clicked on the light,
Or a cloud obscures the sun.

BERT GASS

Saratoga's finest restaurants became that way
Thanks to me.
I slaved and sweated in the steamy kitchen
Of Hattie's Chicken Shack where
Hattie trained me to make the
Okra, jambalaya and southern fried biscuits.
She praised my culinary expertise until
The incident of the turnips and the Winslow family.
Sophie Parker counted on me to prepare the
Canard A L'Orange and Poulet A La Francaise
Every summer on Caroline Street.
Chez Sophie relocated without me after the
Crepe Normande and
What happened to Walter Burritt.
Remember the Red Barn on the corner of
Broadway and Division?
It wasn't my fault that Carl Plant
Liked his hamburgers super-rare.
Last week I thought my poodle would appreciate
A dash of pesto on his penne pasta.
In all of his thirteen years,
Snapper never once sampled dog food
From a can!

LAWRENCE CRANE

In 1991 the County surplus hit one million
And we on the Board of Supervisors
Congratulated ourselves for the bonanza it meant
For the people.
Since then Target, State Farm and
Others have arrived, providing jobs,
Enhancing the tax base, and helping
The surplus swell to three, five,
Eight million dollars!
So why do social services, youth groups,
Welfare and the like feel scorned when
We hand them a few thousand dollars?
Don't they realize efficient government
Is restrained government?
The healthiest synchronicity in the world is
A thrifty populace, thriving businesses,
And money in the bank.

BING O'FLAHERTY

Writing for the Form for forty-eight years
I've seen them all ride:
Arcaro, Willie the Shoe, Pincay, Baeza,
Bailey, McCarron, Eddie D., Stevens:
Give them a decent horse and they
Would not disappoint.
But for the love of the battle and
Exultation in victory, only two stand out:
Angel Cordero and Julie Krone.
Just imagine:
If you staked all your possessions
On a race, and had your jockey do the same,
Promising them ten-fold if they win, and
All the horses had equal ability and
Temperament, and those riders were all at the
Zenith of their careers,
Coming down the stretch you'd see
Angel and Julie pulling away from the pack,
Mercilessly whipping and driving,
And they'd hit the finish line together,
And the "photo" sign would flash,
And you'd wait for what seemed like an eternity
To learn who had
The biggest heart.

MRS. PEABODY VAN WAITE

I first came to Saratoga as a five-year old
With father in 1919, the year of
Sir Barton and Man o' War.
Seeing father's colors of ivory and black
In the Winner's Circle filled my young soul with
Passion for everything fine in life.
Father raced thoroughbreds until 1937,
And Peabody and I ran the stable for
More than half a century,
Until his death and my advancing age
Forced me to liquidate.
With my dearest friends: Alfred Vanderbilt,
C.V. Whitney and Mrs. Henry Carnegie Phipps,
I shared the unrivaled delight of
Breeding, owning and campaigning
Noble thoroughbreds.
Sustained by such recollections,
Each summer I survey the Reading Room
And ponder: What memories
Will these young people hold close
Fifty years hence?

RUFAS PELL

Twenty-seven years I've been comin' to Saratoga.
Shit. Miami to Louisville, Kentucky,
To Saratoga, to New York City, to
Baltimore, to Louisville, Kentucky,
Back to Miami for twenty-seven years. Shit.
Twenty-one years with Max Domingo, a millionaire,
Got a house on Saratoga Lake, one in Kentucky,
One in Miami, and a woman in each one.
Shit. When they're thirty they're gone,
They know it too. Shit.
We got ten horses here already, that two-year old,
He's crazy, he's gonna get himself snipped.
Shit. One thing I know,
I ain't never known one single gelding
On the backside.

FREDDY DOYLE

In winters I grab me a shovel and clear the walks
On Broadway, Division, Phila and Caroline
For the Department of Public Works.
When my back hurts, I stay home.
In summers I work at the flat track
Replacing the divots the horses make
When they run on the grass.
I leave early on days when the sun's too hot.
The rest of the year I stay in my room
On Walworth Street. My landlady says,
"Freddy, you've got to get out more," and
Superintendent Barnes of the DPW says,
"We can put you on a truck picking up leaves,"
And once I heard Rita Costello next door say
I was a fat, lazy bum collecting welfare
Half the year.
One day when one of them starts blabbing,
I have a mind to ask them:
"If your life don't make a difference to me,
Why does my life make a difference
To you?"

CONWAY HAVORD

I was taught
To respect my elders,
Behave politely
And not to speak unless spoken to.
When my friends taunted Wilbur Neevey,
The retarded boy,
I kept quiet.
My friends went on to college, married,
Divorced, moved, died and
Lived.
I stayed in Saratoga and worked
For forty-two years at
Ellsworth Ice Cream,
Within walking distance from my house.
Now I rock on my porch on Washington Street,
Watching the trucks roll along
Unimpeded.

JULIA VOSS

All the new people moving here from New York City
Think Saratoga can't be topped.
But at Stonequist we say Saratoga was better
In the sixties and seventies.
That's when you could walk into Glickman's,
Or Mr. Jack's, or Farmers Hardware, or
M.T. Mabbett, and Mr. Ross, or Ken Rice, or
Whomever was behind the counter would say:
"Good morning, how may I help you?"
And they'd address you by name.
Mr. Jack's, M.T. Mabbett and the rest
Are gone, and living here at Stonequist
At least I have no need to pay
One hundred fifty dollars for a pair of shoes
Like they do nowadays
On Broadway.

MURIEL LAKE

She could have been the next Shirley Temple,
Or at least Brooke Shields.
Her corkscrew curls, her dimples, her
Sky-blue eyes: no one who saw her could resist!
I negotiated contracts for her benefit,
Insisted she keep regular hours,
Arranged time for her to attend class, and
As she became more in demand, her spite at me
Intensified.
Everyone in Saratoga knows the rest:
Her uncontrollable temper, the drug addiction,
Her father moving to the Vineyard, and how
Upon achieving her majority she gained the accounts
I so painstakingly arranged for her.
Meghan, I had only one motivation:
I wanted to share you with the world.

MEGHAN LAKE

I appeared in print ads for Pampers at six months
Because my mother spotted an audition notice in
The Baby Times. At three I was under contract with
Mattel to appear on their toy boxes and then
I had a bit part in a
Cap'n Crunch cereal commercial.
I learned about studios, sets and sound stages,
Bright lights and photo sessions,
Hair stylists and clothing designers while other
Five-year-olds spent time coloring and playing
Duck-duck-goose.
Wasn't it normal that I'd have
Screaming fits, and wail and stomp and throw things?
My career ended the day
I smashed the director of a Polo jeans commercial
In the face with his clipboard.
And now my mother wonders why
I snort cocaine before I drive my convertible
To the Vineyard for the weekend.

TONY LAKE

If I had a son, I'd still be in Saratoga.
I would have taught him to fish, play football,
Chop wood and camp under the moonlit sky;
I would have built him a tree house and
Helped him build an even better tree house;
I would have opened the hood of the Toyota
To show him the cylinders, plugs, and
How to change the oil; I would have taken him
To whatever job site I was on, put a hard-hat
On his head, and show him the way
Contractors work; I would have
Punched him on the arm when he got moody and
Tell him to wise up, and to never let anyone
See him cry.
If I had a son!
After she came Muriel coddled and
Pampered her, and pushed me to provide
More and more for her, and when we fought
She'd run to her room to hide from the
Sounds of thuds and shattered glass, and
I finally left Saratoga and both of them to live here,
Where I run my own construction company.
Now my daughter is on this kick of
"Wanting to know her father," and I want to tell her
How unnecessary it all would be
If I only had a son.

MONICA LEE

Daddy and I went out for a bagel
At Uncommon Grounds and he said
When I was little he'd strap me
To mommy's poncho and my head
Would come to her shoulder and
My feet would come to her waist
And that was so funny because
Now I'm a big girl and
I walk wherever I go except
When I'm tired and when
Daddy carries me my head
Goes on his shoulder and it's
Funny because now I wrap
My arms around his shoulders
And I laugh when
Daddy whispers to me
That he loves me and
He tickles me and
I say to daddy
I love you too.

MICHELLE CLEMENT

Do you remember when I sat in front of you
In Physics class during our senior year?
You'd stretch your legs, kick off your moccasins
And cross your ankles beneath my chair.
I was too vain to wear glasses so every now and then
I'd borrow yours and read the blackboard perfectly.
When I turned to talk to you your eyes would wander
All around my face and I'd feel ashamed because
My face was pockmarked and sallow,
While yours was beautiful.
That was second period. Third period I went
To one class, you to another.
Today I am unaware of the practical applications
Of physics, and the role it plays in our daily lives
Is invisible to me.
Why was it that when you crossed your ankles, the
Left was always beneath the right?

LUKE CHRISTOPHER

My mother left my father before my
First birthday, and he raised me
With my aunt.
All my friends came to believe she was
My mother, and in time there was no need
To expose the lie.
The Postal Service hired me, and
For years I delivered mail throughout
Saratoga, recognizing the writing of
Someone's grandmother, or someone's daughter,
Gladly depositing envelopes containing checks,
Wishing I could hold back the duns and bills,
Knowing the reaction of what was delivered the
Moment everything slid into the slot.
I lived with my father and aunt until
They both slipped gently away.
They never talked much about the past,
I only made conjectures, and
Not a single letter of the millions I held
Was the one I craved.

NELSON PURDUE

As Properties Investigator at
Henderson Hotels, I seek
Existing facilities for conversion
To the Henderson chain.
The hotel in the Spa State Park
In Upstate New York meets our criteria:
Proximity to entertainment and tourism,
Well-maintained and profitable.
Negotiations regarding acquisition will begin
In the fall.
We at Henderson pride ourselves in
Streamlining conversion so that some
Management and staff will be
Allowed to remain, at least for
The transition.
And, to honor tradition, we will
Change the hotel's name from
The Gideon Putnam to
The Henderson in Olde Saratoga.

AUSTIN ROBINSON

That autumn day plays on in my mind:
Yellow leaves and footballs
Flying in the vacant lot
Next to the Schoonmaker property.
Quarterbacking our makeshift team,
Dodging Martin's tackle,
Scrambling from Cain,
And hitting you full-stride as
You blazed into the end zone
Between the pine trees,
Leaving Van Bramer
Gasping behind.
But the game ended,
The vacant lot was
Painted and paved, and you,
Martin and Van Bramer kept
Running and running in a place
Far beyond the football field,
That I've never been able to find.

ACE MULREADY

It was four-five in the third set,
Fifteen-forty,
When I double faulted into the net,
Losing the match to Mitch Lewis.
Like everyone, I began
At love.
My approaches to Linda Levine
Sailed wide;
My volleys to Skidmore, Hofstra and
Tufts, replete with topspin,
Were returned out of my reach; and
My baseline rallies with the bosses at
Espey Manufacturing fell prey to
Unforced errors.
But I keep my racquet strings tight, and
Work on my forehand, backhand, slices
And lobs
In preparation for that inevitable match point
When I freeze my opponent
With a cross-court winner!

SYLVIA RITTENBERG

I wanted to forget coming home from school
That afternoon when my uncle popped up
From behind a bush with his index finger
To his lips. Rushing through alleys
I followed him to the station where
He put me on the back of a freight train
And said my grandmother would meet me
In Copenhagen.
When I'd ask her about my parents
She'd stroke my hair, say "sweet child," and
Look away.
In time I married Herb Rittenberg and we
Tried to put an ocean between ourselves
And the memories.
Working for tailors in New York City,
Becoming tailors, raising children, selling
The business, then retiring in
Saratoga Springs has taught me well:
Six decades and an ocean
Are not enough.

DORA DOW

The wizards at Palio Communications
Pigeonholed me as a little mouse,
Editing advertising copy for the big wigs
Of the pharmaceutical industry.
Being passed over for Project Manager five times
In one year, witnessing the arrival of big-talking
Twenty-three year olds fresh out of college and
Earning more than me never compromised
My dependability. They knew I wouldn't complain.
They were right.
Because while they thought I was parsing the
Willoughby Drug Portfolio I devoted hours each day
To the creation of a web page
Designed to give girls access to
The latest fashion trends
From Paris and New York.
I quit Palio when my web site scored
Twelve hundred hits on a single day,
And now one of those hot shots
Is marshaling the latest print ads
For hemorrhoidal ointment.

REVEREND CHARLES CROSS

Although I'm seventy-two
I feel like I'm forty-eight.
That's what a second marriage
Has done for me:
It's a fresh wind beneath
My religious cloak.
Martha and I had grown stale and
Keeping the marriage together
Because of my role in the Church
No longer sufficed.
Nikki was a waitress at the
Saratoga Golf and Polo Club.
She is twenty-seven.
And now I chuckle about all the old men
Who require Viagra.

MARTHA CROSS

Charles married me fresh out of
Divinity school, pledging a life of
Fidelity and devotion to the Lord.
He kept his vows in parishes in
Oneonta, Ithaca, Governour, Plattsburgh and
Rome.
I don't know if the water is different in
Saratoga Springs, or if forty-six years of
Marriage fulfills a lifetime requirement, or if
Maturity is a pinnacle that loses its allure
In time.
When he took up with the waitress
I joined my sister in Elmira.
In all my years with Charles
I never once made a wager at the track.
Now on Thursday nights I drink beer with
Arthur Tuttle after playing bingo at
The Catholic Church!

CELESTE RINGER

My own carelessness caused it:
I let my prescription lapse and when
I started taking it again I'd missed
My period.
Planned Parenthood directed me
To a hospital in Albany, and
It was done.
But Saratoga Springs is a small town,
And one of my friends must have
Told someone, who told someone else,
So in Church the following Sunday
The Reverend Cross pulled me aside and
In front of everyone said he wanted a word
With me.
I was lectured in his office on
Immoral behavior, obedience to God, and
The evil of sin.
Listening to him, I thought Saratoga Springs
Wouldn't be any worse off
If seventy-odd years ago
The Reverend's mother had done
What I'd done.

CECELIA HAMMERSMAN

Our Ladies' Auxiliary took
The Reverend Cross to lunch at Longfellows
To recognize his tenth anniversary at the parish.
Wine flowed freely, and during dessert
He began making risqué jokes about
Priests in the Catholic Church, and how
Their intimate relations with altar boys
Were nothing new, and told stories that made
Most of us blush.
The Reverend Cross cuts a dashing figure
On the pulpit with his flowing white hair,
But when his sonorous voice
Delivers his sermon each Sunday,
I still hear him telling the one about
The nun and three raw carrots.

SUZETTE RICHARD

For months I heard the car stop and
Reverend Cross would emerge and enter
Nikki's apartment.
I naively wondered if she were ill
Or in need of some form of
Spiritual sustenance.
Then he left his wife and
There was their wedding announcement on the
Society page of *The Saratogian*.
All this time, Henri and I had been in conflict
Over money, and the possibility of children,
And drinking, and whether or not to remain
In Saratoga.
It got so bad that Father Pike at St. Peter's
Recommended we attend counseling,
Wherein we'd be evaluated by
A member of the clergy
With expertise in marital affairs.
I left Henri and headed back to Montreal
After our single session conducted by
The Reverend Charles Cross!

MELANIE ROMAINE

A blank canvas:
Splashes of indigo, crimson,
Olive green: Soldiers on the
Battlefield?
Streaks of pale yellow and
Tangerine above: Daylight
Mocking the night?
A chocolate triangular form
Juxtaposed with a navy arrow
Swirled in shrouds of pink:
Discrete copulation?
Raspberry dots and violet specks:
Freckles on an obscure face?
Squiggly maroon lines
Brighten and expand:
Fingers reaching out for
Heaven?
Let's put the paint aside
And work on the canvas again
Tomorrow.

JEFFREY FOSTER

I was scheduled to conference with
Our tax attorneys in the World Trade Center
On September 13, 2001 to review
Equity distribution regulations.
The attorneys, headquartered on the
Forty-fourth floor,
Did not survive.
For comfort I placed an African violet on my desk,
Then a philodendron by the window for balance.
They were followed by hydrangeas, cyclamen,
Hyacinth, schefflera, begonias and palms,
And in time I brought my flowers home.
I attempt to cultivate roses and lilies,
Orchids and irises, anthurium, dracaena and
Amaryllis. In my amortization journal
Each day I record their divergent colors,
Expanding shapes and redolent aromas.

PHILIP HOYLE

The character of a man, or woman, can be gauged
By how they deal with tragedy.
My associations with the attorneys at
Donaldson & Briggs in New York City
Were longer lasting and deeper than Jeffrey's.
I was as outraged as anyone when
The planes hit, and I will not be satisfied
Until all the perpetrators are brought
To American justice.
However, life goes on, and I refuse
To allow random terror dictate my actions.
The professional practice of accounting
Will be carried on by professionals.
Meanwhile, I wish Jeffrey all the best
In his garden,
Planting flowers.

JARED NICKELMAN

Shooting pains every morning through my back and
My legs, down to my feet and toes;
Crawling to the bathroom, tipsy and soapy
In the shower;
Trying to wrap a towel around me;
Fifteen, twenty or twenty-five minutes
To get dressed; lurching down the stairs to
Pour some cereal for breakfast.
Some doctors blaming a back sprain that became
A chronic ache; others citing
My obese condition; still others hanging it all
On sciatica.
Popping prescription and over the counter drugs
To gain a little respite from the agony,
Now I hear Ball Metal is set to contest
My disability claim.
If the checks stop coming,
Watch me down my pills with shots of
Jack Daniel's.

"Daddy, I'm drowning!"
Didn't you hear me that afternoon
On Saratoga Lake when I was past the dock and you
Looked out at me from your lawn chair and laughed?
Didn't you know my inner tube deflated and
Even though I was barely seven I managed to
Swim to shore on my own and you kept laughing
When I ran past you into the house?
Don't you remember how I locked myself
In my room and vowed never to come out
The day you left?
Don't you know how I waited for you to come
When I graduated with honors from High School,
And when I received my Masters and Ph.D.?
Don't you know I've won awards for my
Building designs, and that I finished in second place
In the amateur golf championship,
And my wedding date is the Fourth of July?
And do you know that when
I see your picture on my mantel,
And think of the cancer that despoiled you,
I have an insatiable urge to shout:
"Daddy, I'm drowning!"

MARY DARLING

A chick bursts from its egg,
"Peep peep peep," look at me,
I'm here! Then come
Brother chicks and sister chicks,
"Peep peep peep peep,"
They're here too,
Look at them,
Look at all of them!
They run in funny little steps
Peep and collide with each other
Peep peep and scramble for food
Peep peep peep and some chicks
Get bigger faster
Peep peep peep peep and some chicks
Hardly grow at all
Peep peep peep and the littlest chick
Watches the big chicks toddle away
Peep peep and closes its eyes
Peep

Peep

peep

.

DANIEL PRICE

Week after week I'd tread the narrow steps of
Caffé Lena, order a café au lait, and
Wait for you to take me to a place
Fresh and open.
Your voice, now husky and deep, now lilting and
Light; your raven hair, now over your
Shoulders, now pulled back; your songs,
Of wonder and hope, grief and abandonment,
Anger and renunciation, loss and regret, let loose
A torrent of emotion that remained concealed
Except for the time I said, "Nice show,"
And you said, "Thanks."
The steps still creak when
I go to Caffé Lena, and as I listen
I find it easy to imagine the
Graying hippies at the next table
Remembering Dylan.

DEIDRA CRAWFORD

Cynthia Lowe is a managing partner
At Rosen & Leventhal, and I am
Her primary assistant.
I have witnessed her lure prime accounts
With tailored presentations, propelling us
Into the top ten Advertising Agencies
In the northeast.
Cynthia's performance has earned her
Bonuses and perks, and I strive to
Match the confidence and control
She exudes in the office.
We drink martinis after work, and last night
She confided to me her secret, her eyes
Glimmering and sparkling.
I came home to Milton,
Nearly shaking with incipient awareness
Of my own potency.

DON LOWE

Success, prestige, accomplishment,
How better to measure a life?
My professional parents: a lawyer and
An educator, large land-owners in
Saratoga Springs and Colorado,
Call to ask why I don't even look for a job.
My professional brothers: a doctor and
A medical researcher, battling cancers
And seeking cures,
Prescribe therapy and medication
To combat my atrophy.
My wife, rocketing to the top
Of the Advertising field, flaunts
The attitude that got her there
And relishes her hold on me.
They pound and pound
Away at me: their success, their prestige,
Their accomplishment.
Late at night, their voices muffled
And their actions subdued, I savor
The supreme intoxication
Of letting go.

DONNA FLINT

You're with Donna,
It's seven o'clock and
I'm in charge,
How cool is that?
I'd let you know what's coming up,
But I don't think I will.
I really like the element
Of surprise.
We've got five hours together,
And when I'm ready
I'll rock you so hard
You'll be begging for more.
So you're going to stay right here,
As if you could go
Anywhere else.

NICOLE HARLOW

Take me to the movies:
A wife with her husband,
Bruce Willis or James Bond,
Rockets blazing, villains recoil,
Self-confidently tough.
We're going to the movies:
A sister with her brother,
Arnold Schwarzenegger or Rocky,
Fists pounding, knockout blow,
Self-importantly strong.
Yeah, let's go to the movies:
A daughter with her father,
John Wayne or Dirty Harry,
Guns firing, criminals quaking,
Self-evidently right.
I've been to the movies:
Colossal heroes winning the hour
Oblivious to minute men.

ROCKY VELVET

It's not the name you used for me
When you summoned me home,
Driving up and down Fifth, Spring,
Nelson and Ludlow until you found me
In my room when you got back.
It's not the name you questioned in class,
Waiting for the answer to the equation,
Or the correct chemical compound, or
To tell me to pay attention.
It's not the name you slurred at
Your parents' house, with the liquor cabinet open,
And joints on the carpet, before we both passed out.
It's not the name you moaned drenched in sweat
In the blackness of a tent
On a steamy August night.
It's not the name you asked other people if they saw
In the days and weeks and months after I wasn't there
When you spoke that name.
It's not the name I regret forgetting
When my name is called.

MACK POPE

Remember the Bloody Marys they used to make
In those pint canning glasses
At Madame Jumel's, loaded with horseradish
And Tabasco? One time
Steve Grayson and I pounded five each
And got tossed out for seeing how high
We could spit on the front window.
Then there was the night I reached over the bar
And poured my full glass of Guinness
On the jackass bartender at
The Parting Glass for drawing it all at once
Instead of letting the head settle before
Topping it off.
Years back I remember picking up a girl at
The Tin & Lint when I said this is where
Don McLean wrote *American Pie*
On a napkin. She walked out
When I jumped on the table and
Started singing the chorus.
These days it's different from how it used to be:
Two glasses of wine at the Springwater Bistro,
And I'm drunk!

PAULA FONTAINE

I always thought that Madame Jumel was
Diamond Jim's main woman, and they went to the
Track every day and the casinos every night and he
Bought her jewels and furs
Even though she was older.
Then Heather Pickney told me I had it wrong,
That Diamond Jim played around
With all sorts of women, and stole money
From a guy who earlier went and shot
Alexander Hamilton and didn't even
Spend much time in jail.
Sue Mooney said Diamond Jim
Didn't play around at all,
Because he was loyal to Lillian Russell,
Which makes sense or else
Why would the restaurant have her name?
One night I asked Mack Pope what he thought
And before he could answer
He belched and fell headfirst
Into the pool between Spit and Spat!

JANICE TREBLEHORN

I tried it once, and I'll never
Try it again. They interviewed me
For an hour: What sports do I enjoy?
Do I attend theater? What sort of satisfaction
Do I derive from my job? What values
Are most important to me? What are the
Qualities I find most alluring in a man?
When I walked into Professor Moriarty's
I saw a skinny man with stringy gray hair
Holding a bottle of beer and
Said to myself, "Please, don't let it be him,"
Then he looked at me and asked,
"Are you Janice?"
I got to learn all about his
Fantasy baseball league, and his
Difficulty in finding a job that suits his
Personality, and why Beck's is a better beer than
Heineken, and if there's one thing he respects,
It's an intelligent woman, while he gobbled
His fish and fries and cole slaw.
When I saw Cynthia Lowe that night she
Grinned and cackled, and said
Those kind of gimmicks
Are set up to drain money from dolts
Like Mack Pope.

SHEILA ORMSBY

Yeah, right, you're an Altar Boy from
Way back, every Sunday morning
On your knees, right, just like now,
Kneeling in front of the Porcelain God,
Barfing up your whiskey and rum and vodka.
And what am I, a nun, St. Bernadette,
Ready to hold your hand or say a prayer
For the resurrection of Mack Pope?
Yeah, your women are all
Mary Magdalene, ready to lick your wounds,
Right, and your friends, buy them rounds until
You're soused and broke, and they're all
Judas when they're gone.
But you're an Altar Boy, right?
On Sunday morning when there's no room
In the Ormsby Inn, why don't you
Make like Jesus Christ and return to
Your father.

ROBERT LIVINGSTON POPE

Wispy white smoke from the chimney in Rome
Heralded the selection of Cardinal Ratzinger,
And signaled the flock to end its grieving.
In the cloister of a sacristy forty years ago
My son lingered long after Mass, and would
Blush and stammer before his mother and I,
And the drinking and deceit were indelibly
Engraved before the disclosure of
Unspeakable acts.
Anger Management brought no consecration;
The steps of AA led away from
The Altar; the bread and wine of the
Eucharist was fetid and decayed.
The beads of my Rosary are
Chafed and worn,
While in Vatican City
Pope Benedict XVI
Offers benediction through
The Resurrection of the Son.

WILL JOHNSON

Close the blinds and bolt the doors:
Who's the hottie in leather boots with
Stiletto heels, fishnet stockings and
Black lace panties?
From a closet a tight bustier,
Velvet gown and embroidered fan!
Into my armoire: where's that pearl necklace?
Oh, those gold earrings and silver noserings!
And how about handcuff bracelets?
What to do, what to do, what to do
With my hair?
A bob, a braid, or maybe spiked,
Dyed purple-pink with loads of mousse!
There's my mascara!
Black lipstick, black eyeliner, what about
My fingers? And what about my toes?
Stand back, let's see a pout,
You go, girl!
Wouldn't they all love to take a look?
Too bad! I'll pounce and purr and
Roar tonight on my own
Private catwalk.

RONALD BERGERON

Mrs. Trottman, are you scurrying to
The Bread Basket to pick up tasty cinnamon buns?
Better hurry, and put lipstick on your cat for
The fashion show!
Eunice and Paul Chamberlain, when
They finish digging up your yard for the
Swimming pool, will you tell me
When the grandfather clock
Does his flips and backflips
Off the diving board?
Molasses in the morning!
If you don't move your feet and flap
Your arms, the planes from Turkey
Will swoop down, down, down
And go up, up, up
When Giovanni flies his kite.
And that individual wearing the pointy cap
And the jacket with the tarnished emblems
Was at it again,
Washing and polishing the clover
Before it opened its eyes.

CANDACE BERGERON

To watch him now, the drool
Trickling down his chin, the legs
Shaking back and forth like pistons,
The thinning hair sticking up from his head
Like straw, you'd never know
How he stood up to James Leary when
Everyone else quaked, how he led the drive
To save the Casino when Congress Park
Was a wreck, and even after he lost the
Election for Mayor, started the petition drive
That led to the preservation of open space
Across from the Spa State Park.
Lawrence Crane, Auguston Blanchard and
The rest revered, emulated, and ultimately
Forgot him,
So they don't hear him telling me and the
Empty rooms about Mrs. Portis
Playing *Clair de Lune* at Convention Hall,
And wouldn't it be agreeable
To see her perform
With Goldie, the parrot,
Tonight?

GERTRUDE FLAIR

Midnight, knees tucked to
My chin, eyes opened or closed,
Sightless.
Six o'clock, dawn out the window,
On my back I see light
Brighten, birds nearby, in a tree,
Chattering up
Daylight.
Noon, on top of the sheets and
Blankets, reaching for
A glass of water, light beads of
Sweat on my arm, the air holding
A faint buzz of
Stillness.
Six o'clock, voices outside, children
Laughing, someone singing, I
Shift to my side, anticipating
Fading light, murmurs and silence
On the way to
Midnight.

PATRICE HOLT

At Skidmore College I majored in philosophy
And found the routes to existential hideaways.
Eternal recurrence enthralled my mind;
I unearthed a will to glory in the circumvention
Of the mundane.
Wild, clandestine battles raged, charged with fury
And exhilaration.
The martial beat of shock and awe
Released my tumult and unleashed
Obedience to an archetypal force,
Spiriting me to the epicenter of battle
In an implacable desert.
Baked by the sun, my canteen depleted,
My grenade and machine gun ready,
Through smoke and dust
I saw two of them trying to burrow
Behind an overturned truck.
I watched my hand quaver as I
Pulled out the pin, and in the
Flash of ravishment
My philosophy
Exploded.

SHAUNA COPELAND

I stood in a valley
You sat on a hill.
I called you by name
You faced towards the sun.
I started to climb,
I needed to see
If you apprehended
What came from below;
If you understood
I'd readily climb
Above all the tree-tops
Above all the hills,
If you had a notion
For me.
I reached the hilltop
And oh, what a sight
Was waiting for me!
And you?

CYRUS BECKER

Broadway, Phila, Caroline, Spring,
Lake, Henry, Maple, Putnam:
Etched with my footprints of forty years.
A purposeful stride in the cool morning,
Watching the women in tailored suits
Lock the doors of their SUVs on their way
To the office.
A meandering stroll in mid-afternoon, following
The girl in the pink halter top until she
Disappears into Summerfield Lane, while
A girl with a blonde ponytail jogs past,
Leaving behind a slight whiff of
Perfume and sweat.
An unsteady gait late at night
To Peabody's, Bailey's, Gaffney's and finally
Desperate Annie's, asking two girls at the bar
If they want a beer when two boys lead them
To a table next to the jukebox.
Stumbling, lurching, reeling and spinning,
Doorways, glances, whispers and motors
Emerge and dissolve along
Washington, Clinton, Woodlawn, Church,
Division, State and Broadway.

FRANKIE SHADWELL

Don't you think someone like me:
My telescope trained to the constellations;
My senses charged by the bombardment of
Solar particles forming the
Aurora borealis; my eyes tracking the orbits
Of Venus and Jupiter; my mind chagrined by
Its role of a bit player
In the effulgence of the Milky Way,
Would have sensed the danger
And escaped?
But how could I recognize the peril
In a body so shimmering and lustrous?
And how could I realize its perception
Would hover above me,
Until I strove to bridge
The unfathomable space?
They can all tell you
I didn't understand the risks when I
Sought the nether regions.
And now the air that fills my lungs
Arrives from a galaxy never revealed
To Galileo.

CHRISTINE SHADWELL

Haul your telescope to the roof and
Point it at the sky:
Do you see tiny
Pinpricks to a world bathed in
Unmitigated light?
Or aim it at mansions and
Townhouses, condos and
Apartments in Saratoga Springs:
Does the brightness beneath a door
Or through a curtained window
Illuminate conjectures and promises,
Aspirations and defeats?
Or twist it around and
Point it at yourself.
Only then you'd need someone else
To peer through.
And do you think your
Magnified appearance,
Huge in your estimation,
Enormous in your conceit,
Would be any less
Indecipherable?

TRACY LERNER

The light from my eyes you called
The Morning Star: enticing and
Mysterious, orbiting the sun
In speed and convulsion, pursued by
Orion, your self-styled persona of
Astronomical mythology. And your
Apparent capture and
Possession of me represented
Your welkin conquest.
Then to see you bristle, discovering
Venus spurns makeup,
Sleeps with her secrets, and
Instead of providing the comfort of
Luxurious heat, impersonated a
Rocky asteroid: unpredictable, harsh,
Arbitrary and piercing.
Your golden aim for a
Sparkling galaxy came smashing to the
Earth.
Did the fading glow of our dissolute sunset
Ignite new embers, and do you
Still ache for rapture,
And the heavens?

GWENDOLYN DUMAS

It's, like, I told him,
"David, you're so wrong,
Like I'm going to wait for you
So you can play hockey,"
And he's like,
"Gwen, we got ice time from
Seven to nine and it's the last game,"
And I'm like, "You said the last game
Was last week," and he's like,
"We'll be done at nine and
I can see you then," and I'm like,
"You won't see me then, I'm going
To Carla's instead," and, like, he didn't know
What to say because he went out
With Carla until, like, last November and
It's like he's afraid she'll tell me
Something he doesn't want me to
Know and I'm like fine, I hope
She does if she's got
Something to tell.

EVA GYAMATTI

They think they know Saratoga, listing
Real Estate like Auguston Blanchard, making
Laws like Lawrence Crane, or saying they can
Save souls like the Reverend Charles Cross,
While they evade and disclaim
The Saratoga I know.
Ainsworth is here, and Marvin, and Sheehan,
And Bronson, and names that they
With their property and laws and religion
Have never known.
Kilmer is here, and Brezee,
Greenleaf and Leggett, Beach, Walworth,
Walbridge and Kendrick,
McQueen, Grippen, Ames and Dee:
Names never printed on their soul.
They believe their notoriety
Is a testament to Saratoga!
Yet they flee from the Saratoga I know,
Cold and shivering,
Afraid and confused.
May they be damned by the knowledge that
All they have witnessed and experienced and
Believed they comprehended about Saratoga
Is false.

MELODY VIX

Tonight was heaven all wrapped up
In a tight little package with ribbons and
Bows and wrapping paper that slowly
Unwound and unfolded and unveiled such a
Scrumptious site and all at once
I plunged and devoured and
Licked my lips and
If I ever cooed I did it then
Before it all came over me again
And I didn't think it could be any
Better but my taste buds disagreed
And down my throat it flowed so
Smoothly and sweetly and
Intoxicatingly that there was no way
It could ever be anywhere near the same
But it was and after the third time
I nestled without a worry without
A motion without a dream without
A witness without a reason to ever
Doubt that this could happen again.

ARDIS HUGHES

As a boy I'd sketch with chalk, crayons, lead pencils,
Whatever was close at hand. Desiring my talent
Be put to practical purposes, my father told me
To get a degree at Syracuse University
So I could become an Art teacher.
Instead, I left for New York City in 1930.
I freelanced, sketched for an advertising agency,
Apprenticed with Saul Tepper, and drew the faces of
Fellow residents of tenements and boarding houses.
Called to serve in World War II, they allowed me
To draw military promotional posters.
I created valiant men absorbed in a noble quest,
I studied faces torn from bodies
Buried in the bloody dirt, and I drew
VE Day on the Champs Elysees.
After the war I kept drawing: crowds roaring for
Bullfighters in Spain; the devout filling Cathedrals
In Rome; faint outlines from windows of
Manhattan skyscrapers; and people
At the Race Course, or Casino, or walking by
The buildings on Broadway
In Saratoga Springs.
In a few days I'll complete my painting of
The Adelphi. Now maybe my father knows
That nothing else matters
If you have food and paint.

LESLIE WARRINGTON

Champagne and strawberries,
Cucumber sandwiches, Chardonnay
On the silken lawn beside the Hall of Springs;
Sponsors, Patrons and Directors resplendent
In black tie;
Balanchine's movements spare and precise,
Soft color and spectacle, crescendo and denouement;
The sky a blast of light and sparkle:
Reverberations of a night of
Carousal.
The gala but one of our
Sprightly summer dances:
A Midsummer Night's Dream we believed
Orchestrated by a mischievous Puck.
Then to raise the amphitheater's
Gigantic curtain and reveal
Discordant rhythms, grating notes,
Stealthy steps and shifty shuffles
Imparting the sea-sick motions
Of pernicious and clandestine
Choreography.

LESTER THORPE

Sleepy newspaper boys, blue-chip CEOs,
Apple-cream faced debutantes:
Watch the fog lift and hear the thoroughbreds
Pound the track while you eat your eggs
On the ancient porch.
Lithe ballerinas and cigar-chomping railbirds:
Watch the bay, chestnut, brown and gray
Breeze past in perfect cadence.
Stout-hearted firefighters and protectors
Of the law: sit on a bench beneath the trees
Where a television displays a track
Only a furlong away.
Ageless actors, opulent owners, testy trainers:
Follow your horse from the paddock and
Find your seat in the clubhouse before
The gate springs open and
Hopeful vacationers, hormonal teens,
Crafty lawyers, circumspect parolees,
Garrulous salesmen and irrepressible dreamers,
Thirty, forty, fifty thousand strong
Raise a cacophony of desire, yearning, celebration
And despair as big and divergent and contradictory
As America.

TRUDY THORPE

Well, if Lester says the Race Course
Looks like America, I can go him one better.
Stroll down our clean streets, dine at
Our cultivated restaurants, witness ballet
In our summer amphitheater, browse in our
Specialty shops and admire the freshness
Of our city.
Then you'll realize that
Saratoga looks like America
Sanitized.

AN ELM TREE ON MAPLE AVENUE

These old Saratoga families,
Tracing their roots fifty, one hundred,
One hundred fifty years,
Seeing the city through the prism
Of their ancestors' eyes,
Have roots nothing like mine.
I was planted in 1831, a delicate twig
When Old Hickory lived in the White House.
A canopy of my cousins shielded
Broadway for generations,
Beautifying Saratoga's golden age,
Before the deadly onslaught of
Dutch elm disease.
Death has not claimed me.
Here I stand on Maple Avenue,
My impenetrable trunk supporting
Hundreds of branches and thousands of leaves:
A living reminder that while men perish,
Nature prevails.

JOSEPH THE JUGGLER

One ball, two balls, learning the rhythm,
Throw-throw-catch-catch
In lofty arcs.
Three balls, yellow, red, blue,
Keep them straight.
Cascade, reverse-cascade, shower,
Yo-yo, columns;
Rings, under the leg, three, four,
Five at a time;
Clubs, off the knee,
Behind the back, double spin,
Triple spin, pirouette, kick-ups,
Fancier and faster,
Covering drops with witty asides;
Knives, torches, risking ridicule,
Upping the ante for a bit more pocket-change
From bored bystanders on Broadway.
Then,
Foot by foot home to Circular Street,
Nestling the suitcase filled with
Flying phantasmagoria
Into a snug corner, secure and
Stationary.

229

ALPHABETICAL LIST OF CHARACTERS

232